THEY CAME TO MY STUDIO

THEY CAME
TO MY STUDIO

Famous People of Our Time

Photographed by

VIVIENNE

With an introduction by SIR BEVERLEY BAXTER, M.P.,
and forewords to the Theatre, Film and Ballet Sections by
TYRONE POWER, JOHN LODER and ANTON DOLIN

Editor:

A. George Hall

Associate Editor:

Margaret Sherman

LONDON

PERSONALITIES

Designed and Printed in Great Britain by

STAPLES PRINTERS LIMITED
AT THEIR ST ALBANS, HERTS, ESTABLISHMENT

Half-tone reproductions by

AVERYS SERVICES LIMITED (*pages 1 − 92*)
ART REPRODUCTIONS LIMITED (*pages 93 − 172*)

Book-jacket designed by

JAMES SULLIVAN L.S.A.I.

PERSONALITIES *(Continued)*

A. George Hall

THIS IS Vivienne's favourite portrait of the Editor.

Margaret Sherman

MARGARET SHERMAN, who has served as associate editor of this book, is best known as the author of *No Time for Tears*, the best-seller depicting the life of lonely members of the A.T.S. She was founder-editor of the *Daily Mail Ideal Home Book*. This portrait by Vivienne shows her in a rare moment of repose.

FOREWORD

By A. George Hall

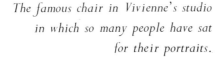
The famous chair in Vivienne's studio in which so many people have sat for their portraits.

THERE ARE MANY famous photographers, but few who can say with honesty that their career commenced after fifty, and that all their famous sitters actually came to their studio to be photographed.

This book records the work of such a photographer, for Vivienne – or to give her her right name, Mrs Florence Entwistle – started her career as a photographer after she had reached fifty. Each of the famous people who have been photographed by her went to her studio, a small studio in Hamilton Mews, to undergo the interesting process of being recorded for posterity by this unusual woman who is really a very great artist.

Some months ago, when engaged on another photographic book, I had before me some prints bearing the signature 'Vivienne'. I was impressed by these prints and discussed the photographs with Anton Dolin. From him I learnt much about the unusual lady whose work I was admiring, it intrigued me and, as I had to have a new photograph at that time, I asked for an appointment.

I have been photographed by many people, including one or two of the more famous, but never so non-chalantly, so disarmingly, as I was by Vivienne. From the moment I entered her studio there was a stream of interesting chatter, highlighted by a gesture towards this or that photograph upon her walls and by conversation concerning some of the ballerinas and dancers I was picturing in the book then under way. There was nothing about my photograph, nothing about where or how to look, or 'please hold still', or any of the exclamations one sometimes encounters when being photographed. A light was flicked on here, another one moved there, and then with a flourish of a hand Vivienne said: 'That will be all.'

I am inclined to agree with many of the sitters who have been to her studio that to be photographed by Vivienne is an unforgettable experience. First of all one anticipates, before arriving, that this artist will be a sveldt, polished, highly professional lady. On entering the studio one is greeted by a kindly, slightly stout grandmother. I am inclined to feel that many of the sitters are regarded with the same care and affection as this lady's own grandchildren are regarded.

Hers has been a most interesting life. Had she not this wonderful collection of photographs to present to the world, her own story in itself would be well worth telling. She was the daughter of George Alfred Mellish, descendant of the great Colonel Henry Mellish of Regency days, a noted artist and musician. The tradition of music and art have carried through the family line to Vivienne. She became a musician, was taught to sing and still – at sixty-nine – has a fine voice.

Being one of eleven children ensured that she would not be spoilt by having too much money expended upon her, but she did get an abundance of culture. Her father took her to the leading art galleries and museums and taught her much of the technique of the old masters, which was to serve in later years both as a painter and photographer.

But her first art was music. Her musical training was one of the great delights of her early life. It was the escape from all else that surrounded her in such a large family. She became a dramatic soprano with an unusual range and had her début at the Wigmore Hall as Vivienne Mellish.

Then followed a not inconsiderable concert career, but her interest in music soon gave way to an interest in art. Whether that was because she met and married Ernest Entwistle, a teacher of art design who himself had a distinguished career, is a matter of conjecture, but it is a fact that she then became a professional artist.

Almost immediately after her marriage came the First World War. Her husband's school was forced to close and he joined the old Royal Flying Corps from which he was invalided in 1918. Then came the beginning of their studio life together.

Mr Entwistle rebuilt his art school in a large St John's Wood house and the studio there became the centre of post-war entertainment with emphasis on classical musical evenings and discussions. Here, among so many distinguished people who were guests of her husband and herself, Vivienne learned the social grace sensed by so many of her sitters today, immediately they come into her presence.

During these years Vivienne became well known as a painter of miniatures and examples of her work were exhibited in the leading galleries. One of these was the famous miniature of Anton Dolin in *Espagnole* which Augustus John described, when it was exhibited at the Royal Academy, as a miniature old master. Among others she did a very fine miniature of Winston Churchill.

In these days few people are prepared to spend the time that a miniature painter requires – they prefer the quickness of photography. To this latter art Vivienne brings all the perceptive quality that she transmitted as a miniaturist.

In 1934 Mr Entwistle's career as an artist was seriously affected as a result of an accident. At that time they had a flat in Sackville Street, Piccadilly, so when the art school ended they started as professional photographers. Vivienne's son Antony took the photographs and she did the art work. Four years later the son – Antony Beauchamp – branched out into business on his own and his mother began to take the photographs herself. The success that she achieved is shown by the photographs published in this book.

In a very few years the business flourished and outgrew its limited premises and she moved to a tiny studio, shortly after the Second World War, in Hamilton Mews. Nearby was an old garage and flat, bomb-damaged but spacious. Here, Vivienne's architect son Clive designed the present studio with the flat above. This enables her to live right on the job so that she can follow each portrait from lens to final print.

Into this studio have come the great and the near-great of the land. The interesting, the people who do things, the people whose names are in many instances household words. Few photographers, let alone women photographers, can say they have photographed three Prime Ministers. Possibly no other photographer can say this. Few can say that two successive Presidents of the Royal Academy came to her for sittings and have been recorded in the splendid portraits of Professor Sir Arthur Richardson and Sir Alfred Munnings, published in this book. Few photographers can have had the privilege of photographing young aspirants to fame and see them evolve as great artistes distinguished the world over. Such has been the privilege of Vivienne, in this very simple studio with nothing elaborate in the way of equipment, these people have come to sit, to chat, to admire the remarkable personage on the other side of the lens, and to find themselves recorded as Sir Beverley Baxter has so ably said – by one who is a supreme mistress of her art.

Somebody has asked when Vivienne intends to retire; she says the answer to that question will be the same answer she gives to her sitter who asks how soon they may have their pictures. It is this: 'You are no more impatient than I to see the film developed, treated and printed. The day I lose interest in all that will be the day I retire.'

I hope this book will be a joy to all who see it. That it will inspire all other photographers. That it will encourage those who feel a career is not possible after fifty. It has been a delight to work with her in producing it.

THE EDITOR.

Vivienne in her studio
with some of the portraits that have helped
to make her world famous.

Sir
Beverley
Baxter

I ASKED SIR BEVERLEY BAXTER to write the introduction to my book because, as a man of affairs, twenty-nine years a Member of Parliament, editor, novelist and theatre critic, he was just the person. When we were discussing it and I suggested that he should also sit for me, his wife said: 'Oh, how exciting to have a picture of his pretty face.'

Well, it is a strong face, and kindly, with very blue eyes.

To photograph he is co-operative and easy. He is an experienced sitter, I should think, because I frequently encourage people to loosen up the facial muscles by talking and while I was preparing to take him, I heard him saying a few words of Shakespeare.

Afterwards we talked of our work and I remarked that I had started a new career at fifty.

'I've had so many careers that I've lost count,' he said.

VIVIENNE.

INTRODUCTION

By Sir Beverley Baxter, M.P.

J UST OFF PARK LANE where the growling, grinding traffic struggles towards Hyde Park Corner, there is a quaint sort of seaside cottage which has mysteriously found itself in London.

Not a sound of the traffic can be heard. A strange contentment comes upon the visitor. Nor is that illusion dispelled when the lady of the house comes in to greet her guest.

I suppose that VIVIENNE has a surname. Certainly she has a husband for I had the pleasure of meeting him when I went there. No theatrical producer could find an actor more fitting to add the final touch of domestic good humour than the man who married Vivienne.

He was looking for a book and I like men who look for books. It is encouraging in these days of television and VistaVision to find someone who reads a book even if he cannot remember where he left it.

Vivienne herself is a motherly, apple-cheeked matron who gives the impression that she has just been preparing a particularly good luncheon in the kitchen. The studio warms with her presence.

For reasons not easy to explain I have been photographed by many masters of the camera. They have lifted my chin, raised my eyebrows and turned my face until by the time they are ready for the kill I feel and look like someone who has been frozen in the Alps.

But Vivienne is not like that. She sits down for a chat as if nothing is further from her thoughts than photography. Then she will say, as if reluctant to interrupt the conversation: 'Let's try this just as you are.'

The deed is done and she resumes the conversation as if it, and not the photograph, were the main purpose of our meeting. As for her husband, he passes through the studio still in search of that book or perhaps hunting a pair of slippers that have gone into hiding.

Yet who can deny that Vivienne is a supreme mistress of her art? If such there be let him study the portraits in this book.

Actually *They Came to My Studio* is far more than a mere collection of photographs of well-known people. London is a vast metropolis but the centre of London is like a village where everyone more or less knows everybody.

Wealth is not in itself a passport to the village although it is not a hindrance. Even beauty is not a sure passport unless it is allied with intelligence and personality. Inevitably the stage and politics are heavily represented because their activities are constantly reported and discussed in the village Press.

Therefore it seems fitting that we should turn first in this book to Vivienne's study of Sir Winston Churchill. Here is the great man as we have seen him a thousand times with all the quiet concentration of a smouldering volcano about to erupt.

He might be listening to the Leader of the Opposition, yet there is a look in his eyes which suggests that his opponent is not doing too badly. In short, Churchill is tuning his mind to a formidable task confronting him.

He never seemed an old man until he gave up office and even then one felt that if the occasion demanded it the burden of the years would fall away. Truly this is a living portrait of the greatest Englishman of his time.

Then let your eyes turn to the remarkable portrait of Princess Marie Louise. It would not surprise us if the photograph started to speak, for Her Highness has never begrudged her friends the largesse of her mind.

I had the honour of meeting the Princess shortly after the 1914–18 war when she gave expression to her thoughts with an incisiveness that was quite terrifying to a mere subaltern.

Note the concentration that is revealed in her eyes. Look at those lips and wonder how long it will be until they speak. Here for once we can borrow the established cliché without apology – for this is indeed a speaking likeness.

Quite obviously Vivienne finds a special pleasure in photographing the stars of the theatre. It is no embarrassment to them when they are asked to look this way or that or to assume an expression which has no relation to their actual thoughts. The actor soars to greatness or sinks to oblivion on other men's thoughts.

Yet Vivienne has chosen to give us Claire Bloom as a young woman in her own right and not merely a Juliet coquetting with the inconstant moon. Miss Bloom's smile in this book is real. One can study it for minutes on end without growing weary or disillusioned.

By contrast turn, if you will, to that irresistible creature Margaret Leighton. Here we have artifice unashamed.

Look at the carefully-placed hand with its long fingers caressing the elegant, delicate white fur about her shoulders. Note Miss Leighton's eyes of calculated innocence, a rich man's darling, a formidable creature assuming a frailty she does not feel.

If we accept the theory of woman's infinite variety where would you find more support for it than in these portraits of Claire Bloom and Margaret Leighton?

On the other hand, look on the brooding gloom of Paul Scofield. Here is Hamlet gazing at Yorick's skull. With the perception of a great artist Vivienne has caught the pensive quality of Mr Scofield's character. I have talked to him in private life as well as seen him many times on the stage, and have been much attracted by his thoughtful melancholy. One feels that his spirit is in tune with twilight and dusk and the misty moon. Not for him the glare of the noonday sun, nor the brawling of the boisterous gale. A gentle reverie has claimed him for its own.

How different is Terence Rattigan! If Terence collided with a bus it would be the bus that would emerge dishevelled. When playing golf he looks as if he has motored directly from his tailor to the course. Note the calculated disarrangement of his tie. Note the handkerchief in the breast pocket with just enough disorder to give that touch of careless elegance.

Obviously, Mr Rattigan is lost in a dream – a dream of box office success. Youth is his oldest tradition, for the years pass him by and leave no mark. Like Dorian Grey, he will never be older than his portrait. Mr Rattigan has chosen, in this photograph, to gaze into the unknown. Perhaps he was recalling the days when, as a rear-gunner, he flew into action against the Luftwaffe, for Terence Rattigan is no mere painting of a man.

But my affection for Vivienne does not blind me to the fact that in at least two of her portraits she has failed to give us anything more than a recognizable likeness. Take, for example, the Duchess of Argyll. Here we have an attractive young woman clothed mentally and physically in a quiet elegance, a young woman who could not be less animated if she were looking at an Eton and Harrow Cricket Match.

Certainly Margaret has the quality of repose but one always feels the mental activity underneath. She is a shrewd observer of the passing scene and a lively critic of the human comedy. She can talk with men of affairs on an equality and, in the process, lose nothing of her femininity. Undoubtedly she can be identified by this portrait, but that is not enough.

Another that fails to give us the person we know is the photograph of Viscount Kemsley. Admittedly, Vivienne has caught the alertness which he always brings to the art of listening, and also she gives us the essential kindliness of the man who played such a part in the saga of the three famous Berry Brothers.

But the element that is missing is the sense of fun and sheer enjoyment of life which has always made Gomer Berry (as he was born) a gay companion.

Most successful men become victims of the machine that they create. Lord Kemsley is the exception. He has a genuine enjoyment of good company, good talk, good wine and good cars. Perhaps his face in repose does not reveal these things.

But in so brilliant a collection of portraits we must not be disappointed if Vivienne, like all great artists, falls short occasionally of her best.

Therefore let us acclaim her for presenting a Peter Ustinov which would not surprise us if the portrait started to talk. For let there be no mistake – Peter is one of the world's great talkers. Yet mixed with his wit and misanthropic philosophy there is a most attractive melancholy. Like Hamlet, he feels that the times are out of joint but, unlike Hamlet, he has no passionate desire to set them right.

Look at the Slavonic melancholy in which this photograph wraps him. But in a moment an ironic jest will issue from those lips, or perhaps an imitation of Mr Gaitskell admonishing wickedness. This is not a photograph of Ustinov, it is Ustinov himself.

Now let us consider the brilliant daughter of a brilliant father. Only the other day I read the speech made by the then F. E. Smith in the debate following the Liberal landslide of 1911. That speech remains a masterpiece of elegant yet pungent wit which never deviated from its purpose. Lady Pamela Berry has many of the qualities of her father. There is the same intellectual alertness just as there is the same interest in the sardonic comedy of political life.

Unfortunately – or perhaps fortunately – politics do not provide a medium in which women can play their full part. It is true that Nancy Astor, Megan Lloyd George, Bessie Braddock and a few others, added lustre to their names by entering politics, but tradition denies to women the high ministerial posts. Perhaps that is why Lady Pamela is content to remain in the antechamber of political life rather than striding on the stage like Joan of Arc.

Now turn to Malcolm Muggeridge, that terror of Bouverie Street and the unpredictable jester of television.

Malcolm Muggeridge is one of those kind-hearted idealists who longs to be an assassin. He feels strongly about everything and anything. When he disapproves of a public figure he pours scorn and contumely upon him, and is only sorry that he cannot plunge the knife.

He is that rare person – a perfect companion and a bad listener. Fortunately he can laugh even at his own indignation. He is a gentle sardonic assassin of character, a sentimentalist with no heroes to worship, a megalomaniac with a pervading modesty.

See how Vivienne has caught these qualities. Cannot you see him listening? And cannot you feel the retort that is about to come from those motionless lips?

Now for a study of marriage in black and white. To Sir Laurence Olivier and Vivien Leigh the world is all a stage, and Vivienne has caught them enjoying a joke even though it may not have been uttered.

So brilliant a pair of players are these two that artifice is almost their reality. Larry can shed real tears when he learns that Lady Macbeth is dead, whereas in real life he would be too hurt to share his sorrow with anyone.

As for Vivien Leigh, she alternates between Scarlet O'Hara and Shaw's Cleopatra and is devastating in either role. The Oliviers are the royal family of the theatre and even the critics are their courtiers.

Turn now to a youngish man who knows where he is going. Peter Thorneycroft was one of the swarm of new young Tories who came into Parliament in the mad 1945 election. He has been President of the Board of Trade so long that he must talk figures in his sleep.

Look at him listening to a denunciation from the Opposition Front Bench. One can almost hear him thinking, 'I could have made a far better case against myself than that.' As a study of temperament under control this portrait must rank high even in Vivienne's gallery.

And now for that Boadicea of the publishing world – Christina Foyle. Her literary luncheons are organized with a terrifying efficiency that brings together the great and the near-great, the fading and the rising stars of the literary firmament, and also the satellites which, unlike the stars, have to pay for their refreshment.

Nothing perturbs Christina. She enjoys the luncheons like a schoolgirl on holiday but her watchful eye misses nothing. Look at her portrait and admit that you can hear her saying: 'This book of Vivienne's ought to make a wonderful literary luncheon for me.'

But where are we to stop in this preview? A preface, like a one-act curtain raiser, must not hold the stage too long.

I have no space to linger over the days when Sir Charles Cochran believed that London wanted good taste in its musicals and paid the price for his mistake – but here he is brought back to us who were his friends.

And now let us end with two famous married couples who lived in the same house in Downing Street but not at the same time. It is hard to think of Clement Attlee as an Earl merely because he was for so long and so completely a House of Commons man.

But the transition has not altered either him or his wife. In fact nothing could alter them. Lord Attlee can reduce a mountain to a molehill and in the process give a curious dignity to the molehill. If an atom bomb exploded he would note in his diary that there was a bit of a bang before lunch.

They are good companions, the Attlees, wonderfully sufficient to each other. Merely to look at their photograph in this book makes me feel that I am eavesdropping. And now let me end my task by presenting Sir Anthony Eden and his wife. It is not a mere play on words to say that politics are in their blood. She is a Churchill and he is of a family that has held high place in the affairs of the British Empire for many generations.

Never in my long years in Parliament did I see a Prime Minister attacked with such violence as when Sir Anthony led the nation into the Suez controversy. Not even Neville Chamberlain faced such sustained hostility or was deafened by so much noise. If lung-power be the essence of debate, Eden should have been brought down like a collapsed tower.

Well groomed, well poised, well informed, he met the onslaught and then led the counter-attack. Merely as the carrier of a spear I was worn out at the end of each day's struggle, yet he never seemed even weary. If you look at Vivienne's study of him you will see that repose which is part of Sir Anthony's strength. He has yet to win the verdict of history but already he has won a place for himself that will keep his name alive for generations to come.

So this preface comes to a close. *They Came to My Studio* – Vivienne's Studio – and by her genius she conferred upon even the least of us the passing immortality of her genius.

And so ends the prologue to this pictorial research of the village of London and some of those who achieved fame or notoriety or even greatness in an era shadowed by the menace and tragedy of world events, but an era that was never dull.

Sir Winston Churchill

I HAD HEARD OF SIR WINSTON as a craftsman in his bricklaying and as a painter. Of course I knew him as a supreme artist with his words. And friends had told me of his impact in conversation – the lively way in which his mind darted to the heart of the argument, the incisive appreciation of the viewpoint of the other man, the quick, constructive swoop on to a new development of the idea under discussion.

But when he came to my studio! He walked in and the whole atmosphere was electrified.

He did not waste a minute. He sat straight down on the seat in front of the camera and arranged his hands – those exquisite hands.

I took two pictures without more ado and then, irrepressible, he obviously decided he must 'get into the act'.

'Do you want a smile?' he asked. I agreed, and he gave me one of the famous twinkles, truly seraphic.

'Let's have a serious one,' he said, when I had taken it and he instantly changed his mood – yes, I am sure, his mood and not merely his expression. But he was back to normal as soon as the picture was taken and he said: 'And now, a savage one.' We had one of those old bear looks.

He rose to go but I asked for just one more. He agreed to give me 'only one minute' for it. Then he criticized me for moving one of the lights, told me he thought I was losing all my effect. I made some calming remark and just went on with it.

That last picture became his most reproduced photograph. He used it as his election picture, too; so perhaps I had some small part in his winning!

A copy of that picture hangs in the bedroom at Blenheim Palace where Sir Winston was born and another copy has been shown on television. When Richard Dimbleby was interviewing Admiral Mountbatten at the Admiralty recently, he said: 'I see you have a picture of Sir Winston.' And there, framed, was my picture.

That session with Sir Winston had lasted only ten minutes, but as he hustled out he was good enough to say that it was the first time he had ever enjoyed being photographed.

It was also the first time, I think, that he had sat for a woman photographer.

Later I painted a miniature of his wife and gave it to him. His delight was really touching.

'I shall carry it with me wherever I go,' he said, as he shook me by the hand.' 'I must congratulate you on being a very brilliant woman.'

It makes you feel humble, having your work praised by distinguished men. It makes you feel your life has been worth living too.

THOSE who come to know EARL ATTLEE, my third Prime Minister subject, speak universally of the great friendship they have for him and of their high regard for his ability – even his opponents, including Sir Winston. But his quality is so cloaked around by that quiet, almost mouse-like manner and those limited little gestures of the languid hands.

You can feel the character, but the outward and visible signs of it are just lacking, except for the expressive eyes. He comes alive most in the presence of his wife. Their great devotion to each other is obviously one of the mainsprings of his living.

Earl
Attlee

Sir Anthony Eden

WHEN MR EDEN, as he then was, asked for an appointment, I was intrigued at the prospect of a personal experience of the famous charm, in close-up, so to speak.

It was all there – the grace and the easy manner. I was at once impressed.

He told me, in answer to my query, that he could stay as long as I liked. Then he went to the mirror and asked for a pair of scissors to trim his moustache – which he always does himself.

The lights seemed to trouble him and he blinked repeatedly. This is not a rare problem for photographers. With Mr Eden I had eventually to say: 'Now please! I want to see your eyes. And I want that twinkle in them.'

He was delighted, they told me, with the proofs; and when, very soon afterwards, there was an election, he asked if he could use my pictures for his posters. It was my turn to be delighted.

There were many more orders when he became Sir Anthony, Knight of the Garter. And most of the large Conservative offices throughout the country ordered large-size pictures for display.

R. A. Butler

POLITICIANS are often anxious to get away before they arrive and MR BUTLER was no exception. He had only ten minutes to spare before lunching with Bulganin and Kruschev. He hurried in late, apologetic and entirely delightful. He was also preoccupied – possibly with that lunch.

Leader of the Commons, former Chancellor, chief architect of modern Conservative policy, Richard Butler does not confine his interest to narrow political channels.

Art lover, he has a wonderful collection of the Impressionists Renoir, Manet, Cézanne.

M.P. for a farming constituency, he is also a farmer himself.

He is no sartorial snob – but he let me smooth his collar and straighten his tie.

Some people do not find it easy to 'convey' their quality, either in personal or professional life. The same sort of thing can happen in front of the camera.

Although Mr Butler gave me his best co-operation, he is no easy subject. Eventually he modestly volunteered that he thought he was better in profile. I, too, had noted that his profile was good – so we took this picture.

Professor Sir Albert Richardson

Sir albert edward richardson had just been elected president of the Royal Academy in 1954 – the first architect the R.A. had so honoured for many years, when he came to my studio.

With heavy-lidded, intensely blue eyes and grey hair, his years rest as gently on him as the many honours he has received from London, Dublin, Cambridge and other learned communities.

A professor for nearly forty years, his gentle courtesy is donnish, only the hands expressing the restlessness of the artist.

The manner is deceptive, they tell me, and he is really something of a revolutionary.

He talked much of the rebuilding of blitzed St James's Church in Piccadilly. Beside his very positive views on present and future, he obviously has a great reverence for the achievements of the past. That is evident in the amount of work he does for the preservation of churches and other historical monuments.

IT OFTEN HAPPENS with men of affairs that they have very definite ideas on how things should be done – even in spheres far removed from their own. It is understandable, but one must be firm, however distinguished they are.

MR SANDYS just hates going to a photographer, anyhow. He may have thought he would get it over more quickly by bringing along a 'candid-camera' snap for me to study, explaining that that was just the right expression.

I laughed and explained that I never copy anything, but he was so determined that I should look at it that he put it on top of the camera.

When he turned his back I turned it face down and got on with the job of moving the lights around. He is a grand person, however, and when he got his pictures – for his campaign in the last election – he said they were just what he wanted.

Duncan
Sandys

Christopher
Soames

I FIRST REALIZED there was an ARTHUR CHRISTOPHER JOHN SOAMES when he took a more serious interest in Mary Churchill toward the end of the war. Before that, of course, he had been around quite a lot on his own account.

Commissioned in the Coldstreams in 1939, after Eton and Sandhurst, he served in the Middle East, Italy and France, and had won the Croix de Guerre.

The appointment in Paris as our assistant military attaché followed and they married in 1947, to raise those four bonny children – on Chartwell Farm at Westerham.

He has had the comfortable Bedford seat in the House since 1950 and served Sir Winston as parliamentary private secretary for three years.

The Late

Lord

Camrose

WILLIAM EWERT BERRY, who came up from Merthyr Tydfil, founded his first paper when he was 22, and rose to the ownership of *The Daily Telegraph* and many other Press interests, died first Viscount Camrose, respected in journalism and far beyond it.

Our introduction was when he asked for a picture which Hugo Wortham had published in the Peterborough column. Lord Camrose first came to the studio with a very bad cold. It wasn't very good. He had to come again when he was better.

He sent a copy of this picture to each of his offices abroad.

Lord Woolton

DURING THE WAR, when I was a W.V.S. worker, they asked me to be supervisor for the St Marylebone section. We had to feed 400 people who were homeless after the fierce bombing of the London docks.

Often, worried over the food, I would ring MR WOOLTON. He was always helpful and kind; and during one talk I told him that I was a photographer and would ask him, after the war, to let me take some photographs of him.

When, recently, I reminded him and he came to the studio, he asked how I had come to be in charge of feeding so many people.

'They took one look at my face and decided I was capable of feeding the 400,' I said, laughing. 'They took one look at mine,' he said, 'and thought I was capable of feeding 40 million.'

Sir David Eccles

Sometimes called the best-dressed man in the Government, SIR DAVID is always a study in elegance – even, they tell me, down on the Hampshire farm.

Despite this and the fact that most people know him best for his work on the decorations for the Coronation, his public work has almost all been on unglamorous subjects – in the Ministry of Economic Warfare, as economic adviser to our ambassadors in Spain and Portugal, then as Minister of Production and, after the war, of Works and Education.

A surgeon's son himself, he married a daughter of Viscount Dawson of Penn.

The Late
Marquess of
Salisbury

ALWAYS A CECIL in the Government. It was a truism of English politics for centuries. And the late
LORD SALISBURY, the fourth Marquess, was faithful to the family tradition of service to his country, to Church
and State, in peace and war, throughout his long life.

Born in 1861, he was 89 when he came to my studio asking me to speak fairly loudly as he was a little deaf.
He was so gentle and courteous and that was the kindly character which shone through all those lines of his
face. An easy study for a photographer, such a fine face.

When we had finished photographing he looked around at my pictures and my miniatures, studying the painting
carefully and very closely. Then he put his arm round my shoulders and said: 'You are a very clever lady.'

I still had a lump in my throat when he was gone – praise from such a great man!

Vivienne is possibly the only photographer to have had the privilege of photographing the entire Churchill family.

— THE EDITOR

I WAS PROUD when LADY CHURCHILL came to me, because she so rarely consents to go to a studio. I believe she came – as she does so many things – for her husband's sake. I had asked to take a few pictures because I wanted so much to paint a miniature of her for Sir Winston as a birthday present. I was struck immediately by her beautiful white hair, with its almost ethereal halo quality, and by her eyes – green-grey, and penetrating – and sad, too.

Randolph Churchill

TO MOST PEOPLE RANDOLPH CHURCHILL seems to be getting more like father every day – and his career has so far covered very similar fields – soldiering and political campaigning up and down the country as well as writing. But he has his mother's wonderful nose – which makes the profile his best angle.

Not a frequent visitor to a studio, he nevertheless was quite at home – even though it was a sweltering day when I felt apologetic about putting the lights on him.

He chats as he writes and lectures – freely and on every subject.

Again, like his father, he has a strong family feeling. When he talked at length about his daughter he felt impelled to add: 'I'm not always enthusiastic about children – unless they're very pretty. My daughter certainly is.'

FAMILY

Sarah Churchill
(Mrs Anthony Beauchamp)

SARAH CHURCHILL is so sensitive and volatile a subject that she is always a challenge to my camera. There is such swift and subtle light and shadow in her face.

She uses her hands a lot as she talks. They intrigue me and I like to have them often in her photographs – as in this one.

Her colouring is as rich as her features are delicate – the hair red, the eyes green, and the skin has an almost magnolia pallor.

Diana Sandys

DIANA SANDYS has a modesty quite remarkable in a woman so well endowed by nature.

She is a wonderful red-head with green-blue eyes and delicate bone structure. Her hands appealed to me very much.

She came to me so very anxious for a good photograph and wanting to help in every way. We talked about music – she has a sweet singing voice – and with the charm of music in her mind she relaxed and we got, among others, this photograph.

Mrs Christopher Soames

ALTHOUGH she is the contented wife and mother, and a complete personality in her own right, I always think of MRS SOAMES as Mary Churchill, because she is so much her father's daughter.

The vitality, the energy which seems never to tire, the subtle spark of humour remind me at once of Sir Winston. And then, when the face is in repose, her eyes quietly lifted upwards, I see how much she is her mother's daughter, too. She is at ease in the studio, but not, I would say, an enthusiast. Rather she suggests the woman who feels: 'Well, this is my portrait day and I'm going to give Vivienne my best.'

With her gold-glinted brown hair, smooth brow, wide-set, lovely eyes, and true wild-rose complexion, I consider her a real English beauty.

LADY ATTLEE brought into the studio the air of quiet fulfilment and efficiency that I had always associated with her.

I wanted to photograph her with her husband – a joint endeavour which they both preferred – and hers was an immediate and smiling acceptance of my pose suggestion.

In her face I was impressed particularly by the keen intelligence of the eyes. I felt that she would have so much that was relevant to say about looking after a famous husband. I felt, too, that she would be the last person willing to say it!

Earl and Countess Attlee

Sir Anthony
and
Lady Eden

I T W A S as Clarissa Churchill that LADY EDEN first came to see me, when she was working in the publicity department of the film company near my studio. She was reserved and shy.

Later, as Mrs Eden, she came for a sitting – still apparently in this subdued mood. She made no request about the style of portrait she wanted.

'I leave it all to you,' she said.

So I highlighted her red hair and the beautiful cheekbones.

Afterwards, when Sir Anthony arrived, her whole personality lighted as he walked into the room. She was radiant as a young girl in love – and maternal as a wife when she straightened his tie for their portrait together.

Sir Alfred Munnings

Sᴛʀ ᴀʟғʀᴇᴅ proved to be the embodiment of the impression he gives to the public – dramatic, incisive, dominant. That is, except for the newspaper parcel.

In the newspaper parcel was his grey top hat. A keen racegoer, he wanted his portrait with topper and binoculars. He had forgotten to put the race glasses in the parcel, but we overcame that minor anticlimax; I found him a pair. Then, while I was taking the pictures, he began criticizing the way I was lighting him. Artists are often like that! I just kept quiet and stood my ground – and he was most pleased when he saw the results.

An Introduction
to the
THEATRE SECTION

*E*veryone knows what a good photograph means to an actor. But what everyone doesn't know is that to the actor the mere thought of visiting a portrait studio sends shivers up and down his spine as though he were anticipating a session in the dentist's chair.

For those of us who work on the stage and in front of a movie camera, the call to the 'still gallery' is an integral part of our profession. The need for pictures for publicity, advertising, theatre displays and newspaper and magazine reproductions is obviously important, and the actor realizes that an outstanding portrait can contribute to his career as does a good play or a fine film.

To the layman it should be understandable that an actor faces the lens of a portrait camera with trepidation, and that it is up to the person on the other side of that lens to either allay or aggravate those fears.

In the twenty-five years that I have been a 'working' actor I have posed for photographers all over the world, and, believe me, there have been times when I would have preferred the dentist's chair.

What is it that turns a seemingly innocent-looking studio into a chamber of horrors? It is the photographer, or, more precisely, the photographer's personality.

It can be taken as a matter of fact that a photographer enjoying a good reputation is an individual who knows his business. In other words, he has mastered the technical details of the camera. But is that enough? I don't think so.

When I first approached Vivienne's studio for some pictures to be shot in connection with a West End production then in rehearsal, I was aware, of course, that Vivienne was a person of great reputation who had photographed some of the most famous people of our day. Yet I was, nevertheless, worried. That old feeling came over me again. Would this be one of those back-bending, neck-twisting, eye-bulging sessions? Was Vivienne a mad eccentric who was going to 'capture' me on film? Would I become her subject or her victim?

In less time than it takes to say 'how-do-you-do', I knew I was in the hands of a 'painless dentist'. And within a few minutes I further realized I was being photographed by a remarkably sensitive and talented person.

As I said before, a photographer may be blessed with great technical skill, but if he or she lacks the quality of being able to communicate with her subject, then all that technical ability is wasted.

Vivienne has the virtue of establishing an affinity for her subject, and, in turn, she creates an atmosphere of harmony in her studio. She establishes a rapport. Her enthusiasm is infectious. There exists between photographer and subject something that can be felt rather than explained. The Italians call it sympatico.

Before one meets or sits for Vivienne, her portraits are just great portraits, but later, after knowing her, those same pictures become the reflection of the work of a wonderful human being.

To compare Vivienne to a stage or screen director may be unfair; nevertheless, for Vivienne an actor will play his most difficult role – himself.

A toast to Vivienne! London's Poet Laureate of the lens and shutter.

• TYRONE POWER

Dame
Sybil
Thorndike

WHILE I CAN EXPRESS with my camera the personality, the character of my famous sitters, I am
sometimes lost for descriptive words. I was lost when I came to write about DAME SYBIL.
What could one say, except that she is a gracious and beautiful woman?
Hers is such a wonderful face to photograph. The contour is so good. Age has given her the lines which
enhance her beauty. Her eyes mirror the wisdom of her maturity and the clarity of innocence that usually
belongs to a child.
This photograph shows what I mean – and reminds me of a summer's day.

Vivien leigh's first sitting was during the rehearsals for her most exacting role in *The Skin of Our Teeth* and I knew the nervous tension that that involved.

But any idea that soothing balm would be necessary was groundless. She was completely relaxed, amenable to any pose and even allowed me to rearrange her hair.

She is an artist-photographer's dream and the fairest of the fair. Analyse her features – the proportion, the relationship of one to another, the harmony, the line. It is hard to fault them.

At her request I photographed her in a new little head-hugging black hat. Of this one, shown here, Gladys Cooper remarked:

'She should be in a museum, for history's sake, as the famous beauty of the English stage.'

Vivien Leigh

Sir Laurence Olivier

O<small>NE WOULD NOT</small> expect S<small>IR</small> L<small>AURENCE</small> O<small>LIVIER</small> to be a most unhappy and reluctant sitter. He looked it when he came in and he remained saturnine as I photographed him.

I realized that, like some other great artists, he could best relax as a character, playing a part. I said: 'Even if you hate being photographed, you really shouldn't show it so obviously.'

That appealed to the workman in him, the actor, and he took off his jacket and gave me the very sweet smile I was waiting for – then several more.

When I photographed him with his wife it was another matter. Her presence made him forget that the camera was centred on him as himself and he needed no prompting to gaiety.

Sir
John
Gielgud

Yᴏᴜ ꜰɪɴᴅ ʏᴏᴜʀꜱᴇʟꜰ watching the fine, artistic hands of ꜱɪʀ ᴊᴏʜɴ and realize again the important part they play in his eloquent stage interpretations.

He was telling me about his holiday in South America, wishing that I could go to see the exquisite colourings abounding there. He was enthusing about it when I took this picture.

When he saw the proofs he rang me to say: 'I feel they are really like me. Most photographers take away my years and leave my face a mask.'

That seemed typical of the high integrity that motivates his great technical mastery of the theatre.

Dame

Peggy

Ashcroft

Photographically speaking, the perfect model is rare. Dame Peggy Ashcroft is one of them. From the start – and she has been to me on several occasions – she showed complete ease and relaxation. Her fine intelligence, her gentleness and winsome beauty combine to make really sensitive pictures.

One day she brought her son – then only four. She sat with him on her lap reading to him so that I might get a natural picture. I was so deeply absorbed listening to her voice and her interpretation of the story that I found it difficult to concentrate on the camera. We got some charming pictures. 'None of these for publication, please,' she told me firmly. 'I don't approve of using my children in publicity.'

Her favourite portrait, and mine, is one of the early ones, reproduced here.

I FIRST MET MARGARET RUTHERFORD when she was playing in *Time of Your Life*, and I found that she was just the same off the stage as she is on. She was breezy, interested and inquiring.

'I know that I'm not one of your beauties,' she confided, 'but get a *nice* picture, won't you?'

She was wearing a gold bracelet that Ivor Novello had given her the evening before and she wanted to show it in the photograph.

So we decided on a black drape and the pose which is in this picture.

Margaret Rutherford

Sir
Cedric
Hardwicke

I HAVE ALWAYS thought that SIR CEDRIC HARDWICKE's voice would be superb in the consulting-room. It has such a quality of rounded reassurance that I find it almost mesmeric. I only learned recently that he was originally intended for the medical profession.

When he came for his sitting he brought his son and suggested that I photograph him instead, he being the more photogenic. I fought the persuasive voice and got my picture of this distinguished gentleman of theatre and cinema.

We talked of his earlier days in the theatre – particularly of the Court Theatre and his roles in Bernard Shaw's plays.

His penetrating eyes didn't leave mine as he talked. When he left I was conscious that I had met a very worth-while person.

I HAVE HAD three visits from ROBERT MORLEY although, filming a lot, he rarely visits a studio. How those eyes shine. He uses them positively, like his distinctive voice.

On his first visit, while he was playing *Edward, My Son*, he said:

'Ah! I see you have a picture of my wonderful mother-in-law.' He meant Gladys Cooper.

You could detect the high regard he has for her, perhaps the awe!

My last news of him was that Joshua Logan, who directed Marilyn Monroe's film, *Bus Stop*, had persuaded Robert Morley to sing – in a London stage version of Marcel Pagnol's film, *Fanny*.

Robert
Morley

Gladys Cooper

THE YEARS have, if anything, added to the fabulous beauty of GLADYS COOPER.

She came to me shortly after returning from Hollywood, where she had been living for ten years.

One feels that her many sorrows have left serenity, but no bitterness – and real generosity of spirit.

Once again I was aware of the very sensitive, artistic nostrils, and the fine skin. She still uses no make-up whatsoever except a touch of lipstick.

I asked her, between pictures, about her life in Hollywood. 'Much the same as it is here,' she told me. 'I have a beautiful garden there and I just garden all day long.'

She looks like a woman who has an affinity with flowers.

Flora
Robson

IN ALL HER YEARS of dedication to the theatre and her successful excursions into films, I have never seen FLORA ROBSON give an indifferent performance.

She has complete integrity, and this is something one feels strongly from the first meeting.

She is an easy sitter, because she is a natural giver. Conversation flows warmly on many subjects, but most affectionately about young people. While she has no children of her own she has virtually adopted many in her welfare work on their behalf.

When she is serious, the face might be only characterful. Then it is lighted, quite suddenly, with a radiant smile and she shines with a tender beauty.

MY FIRST ENCOUNTER with PAUL SCOFIELD was just about the end of the war when I saw him at the Arts Theatre Club in *Phoenix Too Frequent* by the then little known Christopher Fry.

I felt at once it was a wonderful face to photograph, so much modelling and a certain ruggedness – truly like a Greek god.

As we photographed in the studio he talked a lot about Stratford, which he loves, and of his home and wife and child there.

In the decade since we first met he has become a distinctive personality in our theatre – and, of course, in Moscow.

Paul
Scofield

Emlyn
Williams

WE ARE NOW used to seeing EMLYN WILLIAMS with white hair, but it was a surprise to me the first time he came to the studio with it white.

I remarked how becoming it was.

'Vivienne,' he laughed, 'I have been white for years. I just got sick of having it dyed; so they have just got to accept me white.'

He has a habit of resting his chin on his hands while he talks and naturally I had to have a picture of him in this characteristic attitude.

I took care, too, to show the intensity of his eyes – made more emphatic by the black eyebrows.

Diana wynyard is a perfect English beauty. Her skin is quite wonderful – so white and fine in texture.

The soft, smiling eyes are matched by the slightly upturned corners of her mouth, which give her such a tender expression. Her looks are entirely matched with her temperament.

One remembers that throughout her long and shining career as an actress – on the London stage and in her Hollywood films – she has brought an almost poignant sweetness to the roles she has played. While she is first a lady of the theatre it is as the wife-mother in the film version of Coward's *Cavalcade* that I find her most unforgettable.

Diana Wynyard

Beatrice Lillie

THIS QUEEN OF COMEDY came to my studio first in 1939, sat down before the camera and said 'Now make me laugh.'

That is typical of BEA. I had known her for some years, so a current family joke was permissible. As she was finishing her laugh – and it was a good, long one – I took this photograph. It has always remained our favourite.

She is quite composed – if that is the word – in front of the camera. And what people who haven't met her don't realize is that she is a petite little soul. Somehow the rich personality that shines in her face gives the impression of a much taller person.

THE MOMENT TYRONE POWER walked into the studio he charmed me. He is, of course, a professional charmer. That has been evident in all of his films, whatever the role. More recently, we have seen it, too, in his stage appearances. He becomes now, if anything, more of a man of the theatre.

Half-way through the sitting, relaxed, and at home, he said:

'What fun this is, and so easy. I've lost count of the times I've been in front of a camera, but I've never felt as happy as I do with you!'

His only request – perhaps typical of him, was:

'Don't take away all my lines. I've had a lot of fun getting them and I don't want to lose them now.' So he didn't.

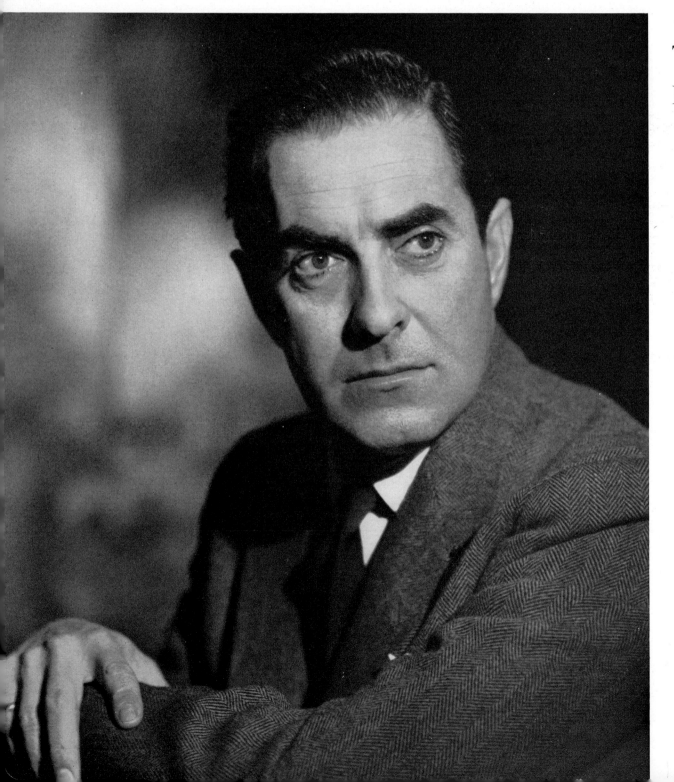

Tyrone
Power

John Clements

MY STRONG IMPRESSION OF JOHN CLEMENTS was of a very direct personality, single-minded and determined.

He is very much a part of our contemporary theatrical life, both as actor and producer, and it is clearly his great and abiding interest. He talks of it all the time.

Both he and his wife, Kay Hammond, shun any publicity about their private life and one feels that the happy stage partnership echoes the very real partnership of their marriage.

Their series of productions at the Saville Theatre was an example of their eye to the real interests of the legitimate stage, linking television to it as a collaborator instead of merely a competitor.

Kay
Hammond

Iᴛ ᴡᴀs ᴀs Noel Coward's *Blithe Spirit* that I first saw ᴋᴀʏ ʜᴀᴍᴍᴏɴᴅ – both on the stage and off.

I photographed her during the run of that play and she brought her fey-ness with her. We chatted about the show – how much she lived it! – and I knew that I must surround her with light to enhance the rakish halo quality of her spun-silver blondness.

She has since shown herself an accomplished actress in many varied roles. In her partnership with husband John Clements, she has done much to help and encourage the youngsters of the theatre – has proved herself as a kind and wise spirit as well as a blithe one.

M ARGARET LEIGHTON had just joined the Old Vic Company, fresh from Birmingham Repertory, when she first came to my studio. She was seventeen years old, very blonde and beautiful and even then showed signs of that elegance which has since become such a part of her personality.

I have always admired her most in Shakespeare – she wears the Elizabethan costume so gracefully, too.

Whatever the role, she appears to live the part she plays and can alter her voice to such an extent that even I, who know her well, find it hard to catch a familiar inflection.

Margaret Leighton

Alfred
Lunt
and
Lynne
Fontaine

IN ALL THEIR YEARS at the top of the theatrical tree, the Lunts had never been photographed by a woman before they came to me.

They are a perfect foil, the one to the other.

MISS FONTAINE's contour of face is a remarkable delight, the line of the chin just perfect. LUNT is heavier, with an attractive bluff strength of personality.

Easy and co-operative, they sat for picture after picture until at last I said:

'I seem to have taken you in every possible position. Short of standing you on your heads, I can't think of anything to do.'

Margaret Lockwood

I HAVE A DEEP RESPECT for people who really know their job, and I always admire MARGARET LOCKWOOD as a competent and versatile actress of both stage and screen.

But it wasn't until she sat for me – and she has done so on several occasions – that I realized how much she knew about the technique of films.

She sat before my camera, looked at my lighting, and altered the angle of her head. We said nothing, because we both knew that she knew the lot.

She co-operated absolutely and we got some fine photographs. She knew more about what I was doing than anyone else who has ever sat for me.

She played Peter Pan on the stage at the Scala Theatre – hence this picture. And on this occasion I really did compose it myself!

WHEN CLAIRE BLOOM first came to the studio she was playing Juliet at Stratford. For one so young she had a strangely elusive air about her. It was the pictures we took that day which roused Charles Chaplin's interest.

Claire's luminous, intensely brown eyes and delicate features do not need the adornment of glamorous hair; the familiar, severe style becomes her best.

She is fundamentally serious and reserved, I think, and rarely smiles. When she does, the youthfulness is there, and that is how I like to see her.

Claire
Bloom

Phyllis
Neilson-
Terry

Pʜʏʟʟɪs ɴᴇɪʟsoɴ-ᴛᴇʀʀʏ belongs by inheritance and by her own special gifts to the great names of the theatre.

She had played with her parents, Fred Terry and Julia Neilson. I recall her as Viola in *Twelfth Night* with Sir Herbert Beerbohm Tree. She is steeped in Shakespeare, has been Rosalind and Juliet, Portia, Desdemona and Lady Macbeth. She has graced Stratford-on-Avon, the Malvern Festival, the Open Air Theatre – and Broadway.

I took this photograph a few days before she left for New York in Terence Rattigan's *Separate Tables*, which was to continue its London success there.

I have watched the maturing of this remarkable woman, whose intensely blue eyes are always clear. But the vitality she keeps is entirely youthful. She will, I think, keep it for ever.

Roland
Culver

Roland Culver has been the gay debonair of sophisticated comedies in the English theatre for many years. It did not surprise me that the role he most enjoyed was Lord Goring in Wilde's *An Ideal Husband*.

He created, of course, the part of the naval commander in Rattigan's *French Without Tears*, and is always happiest and at his best in the smooth, escapist comedy.

When I was photographing him, he happened to be very serious. 'Where is the famous smile?' I asked.

At that moment, my very pretty young assistant walked through the studio. There, at once, was his perfect timing, the famous smile for her – and this photograph.

Kenneth
More

Wₕₑₙ ₕₑ ᵦᵣₑₑᵤₑₐ into my studio, filling it with laughter, I thought I understood why KENNETH MORE had so perfectly played the Douglas Bader role in the film *Reach for the Sky*. He brims over with a love of life and purpose and adventure.

We had fun, real fun, with his photographs. He is quicksilver, and I had to be as swift as he, so that I could catch him in split seconds with my lighting as I wanted it.

But when he talked about Bader he grew serious. 'There is a man,' he said. 'He is all that I could only strive to be.' It was then that I took this picture.

Julie Andrews

Julie first came to me as a leggy eleven-year-old with pigtails. She was having great success at London's Hippodrome in *Black Velvet*.

Last time she came her hair was short and she was off to another success in New York, playing *My Fair Lady* on Broadway.

The years between have given her a pretty figure and a sweet smile, but, otherwise, she is the same, natural, unspoiled.

Lilli Palmer

I T IS SURPRISING how many people have preconceived ideas about how they should be photographed. LILLI PALMER was one of them.

She came to me shortly after she came to England from her native Vienna, when she was playing at the Haymarket Theatre in *No Time for Comedy*.

I took several photographs of her in the position she had adopted naturally. Then I asked her to show me her other profile. She protested quite a bit. But I was firm and suggested that perhaps she had never yet been properly lit.

'Relax, and let me work *my* way,' I said.

She agreed, and afterwards told me they were the best pictures she had ever had.

Phyllis Calvert

THE STUDIO always seems the sunnier when PHYLLIS CALVERT has been there. She has sweetness, real warmth and equability.

I always liked her interpretation of Peter Pan and this is my favourite picture of her. She came from rehearsal with an ingenuous: 'Oh, I've had such fun learning to fly,' and I felt she might, indeed, do that at any moment.

My husband took the photographs to her at the Scala Theatre. She stopped rehearsal at once, not wanting to keep him waiting, and excused herself gracefully to the cast.

She *is* a very graceful woman.

Wendy Hiller

I COULD PHOTOGRAPH WENDY HILLER all day and still want to go on. She is one of my sheer delights.

Her cheek-bones are the most beautiful I have ever seen. But it isn't just her bone structure that pleases. Her eyes are wide and clear and candid. She has tender generosity about her mouth.

She is intense – but completely at ease. She talks about everything under the sun because she is interested in everything under the sun.

This is my favourite picture of her – and it is hers, too.

She seems to express an all-embracing womanhood, daughter, sister, wife, mother. I think the photograph catches that.

A SESSION WITH USTINOV – I have had three – is quite strenuous. Bubbling over with jokes, quips and anecdotes, he makes you laugh so much that you have to beg a breather to get on with the photography. Ustinov cannot just tell you about people. He impersonates them, acting each character to the limit.

I was quite sure that as soon as he left the studio he would give a perfect impression of me – and I didn't mind a bit.

The day we took this picture he had just signed to play Nero for MGM and the contract specified that he must not lose a single pound in weight. He was particularly sorry for himself about that, for the day was really terribly hot.

Peter

Ustinov

Terence Rattigan

I T WAS AFTER yet another brilliant first night – on that occasion *The Deep Blue Sea* – that TERENCE RATTIGAN came for a sitting.

I had been to the first night and wanted to congratulate him. But it was typical of his modesty that he tried to laugh it off as if it were nothing much. It is difficult to make him talk about himself at all, though on impersonal subjects he is animated and has a great sense of humour.

For a man of such talent and good looks he is extremely relaxed and easy to photograph. I like him especially in profile.

Isobel Jeans

Generally acknowledged as one of the best-dressed women of the English stage, ISOBEL JEANS has a particular flair for magnificent hats. I rarely photograph her without one.

She made a great reputation in stylized comedies and has the panache needed to play such roles superbly.

Her interpretation of Oscar Wilde's plays, is, to my mind, most memorable – and she brings into my studio something of the splendid sweep of the nineteenth century.

Mary ure is a typical blonde Scot with a healthy 'down to earth' realism about her.
I photographed her soon after she left drama school and later when she had been chosen to play Ophelia to Paul Scofield's Hamlet.

She was quite naturally excited and happy that theatre and film contracts had come to her so quickly after leaving drama school, where she was awarded the Sybil Thorndike prize.

'But I'm not giddy,' she said, 'and I know I am not a star yet.'

For a twenty-three-year-old that was wise talk and I believe it was meant. My first impression of feet firmly planted on the ground will, I think, prove to be right.

Mary
Ure

Hermione Baddeley

WHEN HERMIONE BADDELEY was visiting me – she has had half a dozen sittings – I never knew whether to expect a blonde or a brunette. She was born a brunette but does not in the least mind changing. It is such live hair, too, a vital part of her and, of course, of her portrait.

She has also the tiniest hands and feet – a size two shoe.

She is an amazingly versatile person with a very ready wit. That wit can be disconcerting at times, especially at the moment when I want her to be serious.

Hermione Gingold

LA GINGOLD, the fantastic, was here in my studio as large as life.

Knowing her flair for bitingly brilliant satire, I had a deep suspicion that she was building up a caricature of me all the time. She seemed to scrutinize me just that way, even while she chatted freely in that deep, throaty voice of hers. For all her great and continuing entertainment value, I shall always be most grateful to her for the laughter she made during the war days with the *Sweet and Low* series of revues.

Dorothy Dickson

THERE WAS ONLY one time, I think, when I was ever a supplier of 'pin-ups' for the troops in a big way, and it was DOROTHY DICKSON who was responsible.

Dorothy had been Ivor Novello's leading lady in many famous shows, until an operation on her throat affected her charming singing voice and she turned to light comedy.

During the Second World War she organized the Stage Door Canteen in Piccadilly for all the services and showed herself unperturbed in handling any and every situation.

For decorating the walls, she rang and asked me for all the pictures I could let her have – preferably of pretty women.

When the lights were turned down for the stage show, the troops would take their selected pictures, roll them up and stow them inside their tunics.

Poor Dorothy, she was always very disturbed and full of apologies. But if the pictures gave happiness to the men – well . . .

Pat Kirkwood

TO MANY PEOPLE, PAT KIRKWOOD will always be the perfect principal boy with the lovely legs and lissom figure. I know that these are among her attributes, but as a photographic highlight, I choose first her lustrous, black hair.

She had her earlier sittings with me when her hair was long. It was from these that she sent off photographs to Hollywood and got her first American film contract.

I have since taken many more pictures of her, with her short hair style. She is easy to photograph. Her gaiety, wit, and quickness shine in her attractive face.

With or without her long black tresses, she is very much a woman. In this photograph I think she shows it most of all.

THIS PICTURE APPEARS at the Editor's special request because he thinks it is the finest he has ever seen of the great ALFRED LUNT.

While we were studying pictures, the Editor recalled the story of Mr Lunt and the lady who was late.

The curtain was up, the first act was under way when the lady came into the stalls. Mr Lunt immediately stopped in his lines and addressed himself to her from the footlights. He remarked on her charming appearance and hoped that she would enjoy the play.

'But', he said, 'you will want to see all of it.' Whereupon he rang down the curtain and the play began all over again! This should occasionally be done in London.

Alfred
Lunt

The Late

Sir

Charles

Cochran

MY EARLY AMBITION was to be a singer and that was how I first met C. B. They were
auditioning for his production of the *The Miracle* at the Albert Hall. They tried me with a mezzo-
soprano part, and an awful accompanist – when I wanted them to hear my top C. They didn't
wait that long.

During the war SIR CHARLES was often on the phone to me, for special pictures, and always
said that he would come for a sitting himself. But it was a long time before, meeting him at a
theatre one night, I prompted him to action; and we got this picture, complete with the stick
on which he always leaned because of his lameness.

'If I'd heard that top C you might never have been here photographing me,' he said with his
benign smile when I recalled that long-ago audition.

Sir Charles died a fortnight after the picture. Remembering the long delay before he came to
my studio, I sometimes wonder if he finally came because he had some premonition.

Conchita Montes

Spain's leading actress, conchita montes, came to the studio when she was starring in London in *El Baile*, the play which made her internationally famous.

I knew that here was a remarkable and vital personality. She is only five feet tall, but has the poise which gives an impression of tallness.

Her vivid good looks are matched by a vivid mind. She is a qualified barrister, a linguist, a traveller.

There was never a dull moment during her sitting, when she fascinated me with travellers' tales. She is the kind of person I am always glad to welcome back.

THERE IS a diplomat's charm about IRENE WORTH, whose love of the English theatre is only equalled by her affection for her American homeland.

I photographed her when she was starring in *A Day by the Sea* at the Haymarket Theatre. I knew at once that I wanted to emphasize her penetrating, deep brown eyes.

She told me that she was very happy to interpret American authors on the English stage – which she did, of course, with Thornton Wilder's *Time of Your Life* in her first London appearance, and later in his *A Life in the Sun* at the 1955 Edinburgh Festival.

Irene
Worth

Dorothy Tutin

AT FIRST it was the elfin charm of DOROTHY TUTIN that appealed to me. Then I noticed a great sadness about her, and a strong dramatic power.

This was no doubt the quality which gave her that great burst to success in the West End theatre.

Her earliest ambition was to be a musician, but acting won through. She was twice turned down by R.A.D.A., and it was that quiet determination in her which made the third time lucky.

After that it was the hard-working school of the Old Vic in Bristol and London – and the critics' accolade for her part in *I was a Camera*.

Sally
Ann
Howes

Even a photographer has whims, and I have indulged one about SALLY ANN HOWES.

She came to me first when she was nineteen and she brought the early spring with her. Her fresh young prettiness, her spontaneity and zest for life were so infectious, that I was as young as she. We laughed a lot and talked a lot and the pictures came along by themselves.

I have photographed Sally several times since, watched her growing up, admired her success and approved the flowering of sophistication.

But it is that springtime picture I am publishing here. I hope you will feel the joy of it.

IT IS ALWAYS a pleasure – and a relief – when a woman has photographic dress sense. They don't all, by any means, and sometimes I have to be very firm and insist on a drape instead.

RENEE ASHERSON is one who did not disappoint me. Her beautiful brocade dress and soft scarf were the perfect foil for her looks, her figure and her personality. In effect, she made her own picture for me. This sure flair for the picturesque is rare. It is perhaps typical of this actress. Her sense and sensibility are as evident in her personal life as they are in whatever role she may be playing on the stage.

Renee Asherson

Sonia Dresdel

Bᴇᴄᴀᴜsᴇ ᴏғ ʜᴇʀ great dramatic gifts, sᴏɴɪᴀ ᴅʀᴇsᴅᴇʟ has, more often than not, been cast in the sinister role.

She tells the story of an occasion on tour when a stranger, meeting her for the first time, said: 'I must tell my wife that I've met you. She thinks you're such a frightening person and you're not, you're so very human!' His wife had seen her as the cruel, neurotic housekeeper in *The Fallen Idol*.

Sonia Dresdel *is* intensely human, with a delicious sense of humour and fun about her. I chose this portrait, in period costume from one of her plays, because it accentuates her natural grace.

Dorothy Ward

W<small>HEN</small> <small>DOROTHY</small> <small>WARD</small> made her début as principal boy she was sixteen years old. The vitality she had then is undiminished.

She is such a natural person who adores being alive, has a genuine love of people – and abounding curiosity.

'No day is ever dull or ever long enough,' is her invariable assertion.

She told me that her greatest theatrical kick was playing burlesque in Charlot's *Stop-Go* review.

'It was so wonderful to evoke a really big laugh.' Together, we mostly talked about family affairs. 'My son is my greatest achievement, of course,' she says.

He is actor-producer Peter Glenville – and I know exactly how she feels.

Helen Cherry

W<small>HAT</small> <small>A</small> <small>REPERTOIRE</small> of redheads I have had in my studio! Actress <small>HELEN</small> <small>CHERRY</small> is one of them. Her hair has, to me, a renaissance fire about it.

Usually there is one outstanding feature with which my camera and I can play tricks in colour – and I want to – with Helen's hair.

But she has another, and more rare feature: a neck 'like a swan's'. I tell her that and she laughs, but it is true.

I took this picture to emphasize the slender whiteness of that neck.

Ella Raines

I WAS CHARMED BY ELLA RAINES when she rang for an appointment – her manner was so easy, so informal.

This American star of stage and screen is the famous daughter of a famous actor, Claude Raines.

She is really very beautiful, and it was a joy to photograph her. I was impressed by her spontaneous praise of other actresses on both sides of the Atlantic.

When we had finished her sitting she stayed for a long while studying the other beauties on my wall. Her admiration was genuine, and I felt that her nature was as lovely as her looks.

Celia Johnson

I HAD SEEN CELIA JOHNSON in *Brief Encounter* long before she came to my studio, but I at once recalled the tenderness and fragile passion of the woman she had portrayed in the film.

'How I wept for you on that dreadful railway station,' I told her as I focused my camera on her serious face and eloquent dark eyes.

She began to laugh. 'Thank you for the compliment,' she said. 'Trevor Howard and I had such fun making it.'

Hers had been a brilliant technical job, and I got down to mine!

Hubert Gregg

Hubert gregg is a versatile Londoner, who could be famous for one lyric alone. I think we can all hum 'Maybe it's because I'm a Londoner'. He has, indeed, published more than one hundred lyrics for successful reviews such as *Sauce Tartare*, *Strike a New Note*, and the wartime *Sweet and Low*.

An easy conversationalist with rugged good looks, I found him a very pleasant sitter who did not mind the lights.

He is, of course, an accomplished actor. He came up in the theatre through repertory, has played at the Open-air Theatre and on the West End stage. With his wife, Pat Kirkwood, he did a popular family series for the radio.

Arthur Macrae

Arthur macrae, author, actor and bachelor, came to the studio when his celebrated comedy *Traveller's Joy* was being revived for television.

He has much charm, a subtle sense of humour and likeable modesty for such a brilliant actor. His writing has something of Noel Coward about it – and he plays a Coward role with the wit and sophistication it requires.

I find him very good looking and a true photogenic subject – his looks and his voice remind me of the late Gerald du Maurier.

An Introduction to the FILM SECTION

*W*hen Vivienne asked me to write a foreword for the Film Section of her book, I looked around the walls of her studio covered with famous personalities, and was surprised and flattered. Her answer as to why I should be asked to embark upon this pleasant task was typical of her: 'Because you know your trade, John.'

Yes, I think she's right about that one, having been at it since 1928! Like all actors, I have had to learn it the hard way, from dress extra to star, bit player to feature player, from somewhat callow youth to what is now a somewhat mellow and mature middle-age. There is no short cut to success in our business and there are many disappointments and frustrations. This is also very true about Vivienne's business. Here, also, the knowledge of one's trade is of vital importance. Sometimes I think the actor and the actress don't attach the value they should to the still and portrait photographer, yet what is almost the first question we are asked when we go to be interviewed by producer, director or casting director: 'Can I see your photograph?' Sometimes I wonder how far we would get without those photographs.

The general public does not realize the important part that the portrait photographer plays in studio life. Every contract player in every major studio in Hollywood has a portrait sitting every four or five months, and, also, after each film has been made the cast is photographed in the portrait gallery. These pictures are then distributed to the Press for publicity purposes and shown outside theatres and cinemas. It goes without saying that these photographs must be somewhere near the acme of perfection, for they help to sell tickets.

I have been photographed by some of the top experts in Hollywood, Paris, London and New York, and Vivienne's technique is of the best. There is no fuss with setting lights or posing, no temperamental flurries. You just sit down in a chair, relax, and have a chat. Before you realize it, thirty to forty pictures have been taken. That is the way the really great ones work, and it seldom fails to produce results. Also with Vivienne there is very little retouching. She lights you properly in the first place and leaves it at that. As a result you get a portrait with character, not an emasculated, washed-out picture the sole aim of which is flattery.

Yes, Vivienne knows her trade all right – and I am happy and flattered to be the one that she has chosen to write a foreword on what is an extremely interesting section of her book.

John Loder.

JOHN LODER

DAVID NIVEN came in with his usual smiling charm. I took several serious studies, but I could not resist his smile.

'I've enjoyed this,' he said, when he was leaving. 'Indeed, I hope you've made a mistake and not put any film in the camera – so I'll have to come to the studio and have the session all over again.'

He has, and I think he always will have, a boyishness about him that rouses the maternal instinct in most women. This picture shows that boyishness and is my favourite photograph of him.

David
Niven

John Mills

I T NEEDS a bit of persuasion to get JOHN MILLS to a private studio. He is another of those sensitive, nervous actors who just isn't at home before the camera unless he is playing a part.

His stage and film career have been in the top flight, but I could not draw him out on that.

I tried family talk and then he relaxed a little, happy to be talking about his playwright wife, Mary Hayley Bell.

But my pictures were still not coming the way I wanted them. He did not seem to know what to do with his hands. Then:

'Can I smoke?' he said – and, of course, he did. After that it was easy.

WHEN ANOTHER portrait photographer's wife – especially when the photographer is Cornel Lucas – came to my studio with: 'He's been on at me for weeks to come to you. He says you take real pictures,' I preened a little.

BELINDA LEE is, of course, a photographer's joy, completely adaptable.
Her mass of blonde hair has such natural beauty and with a mere shake of the head it seems to fall into any shape required.

With her fine bone structure, she has a loveliness that will not fade.

Belinda
Lee

Jack
Hawkins

JACK HAWKINS was having a morning free from filming *Fortune is a Woman*, the Launder and Gilliat production, with Arlene Dahl.

Looking intently at the camera he suddenly asked me: 'What stop do you use?'

'I haven't the faintest idea!' I countered. 'The camera just does as I tell it.'

Informally sweatered, intensely masculine, with an almost austere strength in his face, I could understand why for so many film-goers he remained the stern naval commander of *The Cruel Sea*.

But rather wistfully he told me that he was trying to forget uniforms. 'I haven't been in service dress for four years,' he said.

When he smiled his wonderful smile and his eyes crinkled with laughter, I could see that he would be equally at home in any civilian role.

Jean Kent

There is something of the Gaiety Girl in JEAN KENT—a warmth and vivacity and generosity—which would account for her sympathetic interpretation of 'Trottie True' in the film of that name.

But she didn't have anything to say about films or stage or television. Instead we talked about food, a subject in which we both take a connoisseur's interest.

Down on her Boxford farm—and farming is another of her keen interests—her friends make straight for the kitchen, not only to eat, but to look through her amazing collection of cookbooks.

'Can you prepare Albanian dishes?' I asked her. 'I can now,' she grinned. 'My husband, Yusuf, taught me.'

Dawn Addams

One of the rewards of my job is that some of my pictures have helped young people to fame. DAWN ADDAMS is one of them.

She came to me first when she was only eighteen, or not much more; an enchanting child; she then needed guidance before the camera—a little pruning one might call it.

Her eyes are the bluest of blue with a constant twinkle, so that it doesn't matter if they are slightly on the small side. Her nose is angelic, a gift to a photographer. And her mouth is frankly beautiful.

She sent the photographs to her father in New York who posted them off to Hollywood—and back came a contract for her first film.

In the modern fairy tale manner she soon married an Italian Prince—Vittorio Massimo.

Virginia McKenna

HERE IS A NATURAL BLONDE with blue eyes and lovely poise. This was her first photograph in London, taken after H. M. Tennent Ltd had discovered her in repertory and presented her to the West End stage in 1949.

Since then she has gone from strength to strength. On stage she has played with the Old Vic and been in plays with Diana Wynyard, Gielgud, Scofield and others.

She won the television award for her Juliet in *Romeo and Juliet* in 1955 and the following year marked up a big film success, co-starring with Peter Finch in Nevil Shute's *A Town Like Alice*.

Genevieve Page

THIS BEAUTIFUL blue-eyed blonde actress of stage and films, who grew up in Paris under the German occupation, came to me when she was making her first British film, a comedy, with David Niven.

She arrived with a shoulder-length 'page-boy' hair-do and she converted it in a twinkling to the upswept Edwardian style. She can do literally anything with her hair. She just picks it up and pins it. No top hairdresser could do better.

She has, too, a most entrancing smile.

Donald
Gray

Donald gray has such a wonderful profile that I could well understand the story of husbands bombarding the B.B.C. with protests that he was too handsome for television.

Tall, dark-haired, with deep-set grey eyes, he would be many a housewife's choice, I should imagine. Gray is a South African who came to England and was just getting his start in films when the war came.

It was soon after he landed in Normandy on D-Day that he was wounded and lost his left arm. But he was determined to get back into acting and it is remarkable how naturally he has managed his artificial arm since then.

My last news of him was that he was making a series of films for American television – playing the part of a one-armed detective.

Stephen Boyd

WHEN I first saw STEPHEN BOYD in the film *The Man Who Never Was*, I thought what a wonderfully strong face he had.

In the studio he was great fun. He seemed to regard life as one huge joke. He told me how he had taken various jobs, between acting, including one as a cafeteria attendant, and how he never wanted to pour another cup of coffee.

He had also busked in Leicester Square one night with his guitar and made a pound and sixpence.

'I blew the lot on one meal,' he told me in his Irish-Canadian lilt, 'the most memorable meal of my life.'

I should think the days of unemployment and hunger are behind him now, however, for he has had plenty of stage experience in America, Ireland and English repertory and his film success seems assured.

It was quite a shock when RICHARD TODD walked in. I was expecting a very tall man and I found him only of average height.

It must have been that strong personality, the breadth of vision which he portrayed in his films, which had given me that impression. He seemed 'tall' again when we talked.

He was very quiet and very reserved, though he gainsayed a smile now and then.

I knew that he was one of those rare people who rocketed to film fame – and stayed famous.

Before he left the studio I thought I knew why.

His is a wonderful profile – and this the most interesting study I took.

Richard Todd

John
Loder

Aᴏᴜᴛᴇʀ ᴀ ᴅᴇᴄᴀᴅᴇ in Hollywood and on Broadway, ᴊᴏʜɴ ʟᴏᴅᴇʀ returned to London still the same handsome, so very English, old Etonian.

His long and lime-lighted career has given him a mellow gentleness and his manly courtesy makes meeting him a memorable pleasure.

When I photographed him – such a natural sitter – he was working on the film *Esther Costello* with Joan Crawford. He has worked with Bette Davis, co-starred in the United States with Gertrude Lawrence and was once a fellow extra with Marlene Dietrich in Berlin – for which they were paid five marks a day!

'The truly great stars are the most easy to work with,' he said. 'The difficult ones are the ambitious little starlets.'

I asked him which of the stars he remembered best from his earliest days. He smiled and said: 'I think perhaps Rin-Tin-Tin. I was in his first talking, or should I say "barking" picture.'

Maureen Swanson

MAUREEN SWANSON is among my loveliest young sitters, and a very graceful one. It is something of that grace which I find most marked in dancers who are ballet-trained.

Her green eyes sparkle, her raven hair has a soft lustre, and that pretty mouth has an easy smile. She has lived very fully in her twenty-three years. She told me that she was on the stage at the age of twelve, up in Glasgow where she was born. Since then, of course, she has been seen often on television, dancing with the Sadlers Wells company, and latterly in films.

Shirley Eaton

EVEN AT FOURTEEN, when she first came for a sitting, SHIRLEY EATON was a very pretty child.

At nineteen, and Mr Rank's latest star, she had become quite a beauty. Her hair is really golden, the eyes intensely blue beneath well-defined, wing-like eyebrows.

I did not care for the jersey she was wearing when she came for this picture. So I took it straight off and put lace around her shoulders.

Rossano Brazzi

N O MOVIE-CAMERA and make-up tricks would be necessary for Italian film star ROSSANO BRAZZI. He really is unbelievably handsome in the flesh.

I was rather glad to see the pepper-and-salt of his hair – it made him a little more real!

Making his first film in England – *Esther Costello*, with Joan Crawford – he came round one Sunday morning and we talked about week-end, homely things.

Signor Brazzi told me that he had been married for seventeen years. 'Happy marriage keeps the head from turning when one has this screen success,' he said richly in Italianate English.

Mel Ferrer

Mᴇʟ ꜰᴇʀʀᴇʀ came to me, before he married Audrey Hepburn, while he was making a film called *Lili*. I asked him what he did in the film.

'Mostly look at Lili,' he said.

He is very tall and most charming. And we had a lot of fun between the pictures.

Photographically he is interesting. There is a bright twinkle in his eye one moment and the saddest look the next — it is a face full of character.

It was very satisfying to succeed in catching so many of the fleeting expressions in such a mobile subject.

An Introduction
to the
BALLET SECTION

*P*erhaps *of all the many famous names in politics, society, screen, stage and ballet, I can say that I have known Vivienne longer than any one of those pictured in this book of photographic achievement and pictorial beauty.*

Nearly thirty years ago she painted a small miniature of me in my dance 'Espagnol'. Then I could have bought it for ten pounds. I did not have ten pounds to buy it. Now I do not have the £200 for which she might sell it to me.

Let me at once confess or acknowledge the fact that though I have been photographed some thousands of times, it is rarely an experience I enjoy. I do not relish the candid camera at any time especially action photographs of ballet and ballet dancers. I find in most instances they are quite horrible, distorted, and somehow always manage to be taken at the wrong moment.

How right and how clever the divine Anna Pavlova was never to allow, with her knowledge or per-mission, an action photo. I agree that perhaps from the balletic history of the dance, much may have been lost by her adamant decision and much has been stored up for the future by the dancers of today who really seem to have no choice in the matter.

Vivienne's posed photographs are, to me, real, and convey the intrinsic qualities of the dance. They capture the magic of a Markova; the grandeur of a Fonteyn.

ANTON DOLIN

Alicia
Markova

Markova rang me one morning as eager as a child to ask if she might run in to be photographed in her new garden-party frock. We took some light-hearted pictures.

She is one of my most frequent sitters and doesn't mind how many pictures I take. In fact, one feels her real enjoyment and that is added pleasure to me.

But I like most to photograph her as Giselle, which is her special ballet. Her hands alone are expressive of her whole mood.

She has grace and beauty at all times. In the absolute stillness of her repose, her beauty is ineluctable.

Dame
Margot
Fonteyn

MARGOT FONTEYN, now wife of the Panamanian Ambassador in London, Dr Roberto Arias, came to me the day after she had been made a Dame Commander of the Order of the British Empire.

Although she has been acclaimed the world's greatest ballerina she has remained completely unspoiled.

We had great fun during her sitting. When I'm moving the lights I always chat out loud, telling myself what I am doing. I laughed to Margot: 'Take no notice, I can't work in silence.'

She laughed back: 'I was adoring it all, because that is me. I just can't pack my trunks for a journey unless I say aloud to myself all the things I want.'

Anton
Dolin

I HAVE KNOWN the wealth of vitality and inexhaustible energy that ANTON DOLIN has had since he was eighteen. He didn't know, then, that I was to become the photographer for whom he would sit so often. Our first was as St George in *Where the Rainbow Ends*, and there have been many other ballet pictures since.

He is the most unstinting giver, both spiritually and materially – and how many fellow artists have told me that, but he, never. Yet he retains a deep reticence of self, which perhaps is only revealed in his dancing. My picture of him, with Markova, in *Giselle* shows the artist in perfection. This picture as St George is one that is so much admired that it must appear here.

The PREMIER DANSEUR of London's Festival Ballet, JOHN GILPIN, moves with the easy supple grace you would expect in one who has been trained as a dancer since he was seven.

He has been to me for about ten sittings, mostly in costume, and he is very easy to photograph.

Although he has danced with many great ballerinas – including Markova, Danilova, Slaveska, Riabouchinska, Chauvire and Krassovska – he seemed completely excited about the thrill of dancing with Margot Fonteyn at Monte Carlo during the Christmas season of 1955.

Five years' travelling with the Ballet Rambert and six with the Festival Ballet, has built for him a great international reputation.

He is today recognized by most people competent to judge, as the leading male dancer of the Western world.

John
Gilpin

As a principal soloist with the Sadler's Wells Ballet, philip chatfield has won particular praise for his interpretation of the poet in *Les Sylphides*.

I was aware of the sensitivity in this rather tall dancer. He is obviously dedicated to his art, with little time for extraneous interests – though he told me with some pride that he is godfather to a baby boy called Leslie!

After early training at Southampton he was with the Sadler's Wells School for four years, and then joined the Company.

He frequently dances principal roles in the classical ballets – among them Prince Siegfried in *Lac des Cygnes*. He partners lovely ballerina Beryl Grey.

Philip
Chatfield

Michael Somes

THE SADLER'S WELLS company's principal male dancer, MICHAEL SOMES trained exclusively with that company's school from the age of fifteen.

He first attracted attention with his remarkable elevation and ballon, which Frederick Ashton used finely in *Horoscope* and in *The Wanderer*.

He returned to the company in 1945 after four years in the Army and gave a brilliant performance in Ashton's new work, *Symphonic Variations*.

Besides his classic work he has more recently created roles in *Rinaldo and Armida*, *La Peri* and *Birthday Offering*. He is, however, known to most people as the partner in many great ballets of Dame Margot Fonteyn.

Dame
Ninette
de Valois

W<small>HEN</small> <small>NINETTE DE VALOIS</small> sat down in my studio, it was as if she were alone in a box at Covent Garden, watching her company, oblivious to all but the movement she saw.

'That is just it,' I told her – and took this photograph.

Dame Ninette has beautiful composure. The hands are telling, the eyes, heavy-lidded, show deepest concentration.

Somehow, complete knowledge and passionate love for her art emanate from this gracious woman, to whom the English ballet owes its entity more than to any other one person.

Dame Adeline Genee

WHEN DAME ADELINE GENEE came to sit for me, she was wearing an exquisite diamond brooch which glinted rainbow colours under the lights.

'Queen Alexandra gave this brooch to me,' she said tenderly. 'It is one of my greatest treasures.'
This gracious, unspoilt lady recalled so eloquently the richness of those Edwardian times.

Her name immediately conjures up the days of the Alhambra in Leicester Square and the old Empire, when she was doing so much to make ballet popular in Britain.

She has an abiding place in our ballet, symbolized by the Adeline Genee gold medal. Another of my sitters, John Gilpin, won this medal when he was thirteen. He nearly missed the award on the ground that he was too young. It was, I believe, Marie Rambert, who swung the examiner's vote.

Belinda
Wright

Lovely belinda wright is a superlative Swanhilda in the Festival Ballet's *Coppelia*. I love her, too, when she portrays the wide-eyed innocence of Alice.

Anton Dolin was there when Belinda came along and he saw a little Victorian chair which gave us the idea of setting the scene for an *Alice in Wonderland* shot – with a table built up of stools and a board.

This ballerina has the quality of conveying freshness and gamin lightness. In classic roles it becomes an ethereal quality which recalls Markova.

To meet she is quite a practical young woman, quiet and matter-of-fact in the midst of her many artistic interests.

A VERY PRETTY GIRL, with long black hair drawn back smoothly into a chignon, MARILYN BURR first came to me at one of the major turning points of her life.

Daughter of a Sydney dancing teacher, she had come to London as the focal point of ballet. About all she had found was disappointment, even disillusion – and two shows a day in the Palladium pantomime chorus.

Then she joined the *corps de ballet* at the Festival Ballet and within a few weeks was given the chance to replace the injured Krassovska in *The Black Swan pas de deux*.

Since then she has emerged as a considerable virtuosa with a strong personality. She is now one of the principal ballerinas of the Festival Ballet Company.

Marilyn
Burr

Anton dolin brought mr and mrs harald lander to my studio when he was producing that amazing piece of virtuosity, *Etudes*, which Harald created for the Royal Danish Ballet.

When he brought it to London, with his wife as principal ballerina, she achieved one of those amazing successes such as are hardly ever heard of.

She is a lovely girl, quite unspoilt, with a genuine modesty that is almost shyness.

She had gone into ballet school in childhood against the reluctance of her parents; and in Copenhagen progress for all dancers was slowed because the ballet had to take its turn with opera.

But in Paris she had the chance to study with the best teachers and make occasional guest appearances. This and her tours with the Festival Ballet have developed her style.

She is a romantic ballerina of dignity, graciousness and promised greatness.

Toni Lander

Svetlana Beriosova

Her thoughtful eyes and expressive eyelids are a compelling feature in beriosova's sensitive face.

She has a natural charm, fragile grace – and continental chic.

To me she was another heart-warming reminder of the great comradeship that exists in the ballet world.

She talked almost all the time of other ballerinas at Sadler's Wells, remembering too, the friends she had made with the Grand Ballet de Monte Carlo and with the Metropolitan Ballet, of which she was prima ballerina.

Wʜᴇɴ ʙᴇʀʏʟ ɢʀᴇʏ came she had just heard that Violetta Elvin was leaving ballet to marry and live in Rome and she was very sad.

They had shared a dressing-room for ten years, she said, and had never had a cross word. I noticed that, as with other ballerinas – they all seem to be so warm-hearted.

Beryl Grey talked a lot about her small son, aged two. She said she was learning from him, particularly the art of absolute concentration.

She herself had begun dancing tuition at four, graduated to the Sadler's Wells company at fourteen and danced Odette/Odile in *Lac des Cygnes* on her fifteenth birthday.

Beryl
Grey

Moira shearer first came to me when she was dancing at Covent Garden, and I photographed her in her Cinderella costume. I took more pictures, before her marriage to Ludovic Kennedy, at Hampton Court Palace. My last pictures are of her with her husband and little daughter Ailsa.

Although she is a fine dancer and actress, I enjoyed most of all photographing her *en famille*. She is so delightful with her husband and true family devotion is immediately apparent and very moving.

She is another gift to photography. With her graceful ballet movement she poses so naturally.

Her hair, which is the highlight to me, has a glow about it one can almost feel as well as see.

Moira Shearer

David
Blair

Dᴀᴠɪᴅ ʙʟᴀɪʀ is known to most ballet enthusiasts for his magnificent interpretation of the Bluebird in *Sleeping Princess*. Regarded by many as one of the very great dancers, he shines in many of the leading roles at Covent Garden and wherever the Sadler's Wells company dances.

He trained at the Sadler's Wells School, then became a principal dancer with the Sadler's Wells Theatre Ballet and joined the Company in 1953 as a principal soloist.

Always an admirer of his dancing, I was impressed by his amazing physique when he came to the studio. I was reminded of the classical Greek statue of the discus thrower.

When he had found his pose for a picture he didn't move a muscle as I arranged the lights; there was that statue quality again.

Myles
Marsden

KNOWING ANTON DOLIN's skill and unerring instinct in 'finding' young dancers, I looked
forward to meeting MYLES MARSDEN.

I noticed the rhythm and melody in his movement when he came to me with Anna Roya.

Dolin had auditioned him in London and sent him to Anna Roya's International Ballet School
at Split, in Yugoslavia, for four years' training.

With another year's training ahead, he came to London to see the Festival Ballet's *Giselle*, especially
to watch Anton Dolin's interpretation of Albrecht.

He had already danced Mercutio in *Romeo and Juliet*, and the devil in *The Devil and the Village*,
when they were produced in Yugoslavia.

Dolin is confident that Marsden will make a fine future Albrecht.

Flemming Flindt

Only twenty, Flemming Flindt is already a principal dancer with the Festival Ballet, combining a natural grace with a determined masculinity that is characteristically Danish.

He has a breezy sense of humour, but he is obviously most serious about his career. After graduating from the Royal Danish Ballet School to the State company, he came to England on a four-year leave of absence so that he would have an earlier chance to dance principal classic roles.

Any criticisms of England? Two. The grime of some of our provincial cities – which is natural in a Dane – and the food – which could be expected from the son of a Copenhagen *restaurateur*.

Brian Shaw

Brian Shaw joined the Sadler's Wells Ballet Company after he left the Services and has since then become one of its most important dancers in both classical and character roles.

In a company with about fifty ballets in its repertoire, his versatility must be most useful, and he has danced a score of leading roles, from the dancing master in *Rake's Progress* to one of the partners in *Birthday Offering*.

Anna Roya

Aɴɴᴀ ʀᴏʏᴀ was in England studying that supreme display of a ballerina's mime and technical ability, the role of Giselle, in the choreography and production of Anton Dolin's version of the great classical ballet.

Her brilliant young protégé, Myles Marsden, was with her – he had been studying at her ballet school in Belgrade – and I suggested some pictures together.

Shortly after this photograph was taken Miss Roya and Myles Marsden danced Giselle in Split, Yugoslavia, in the presence of Anton Dolin.

Violetta Elvin

Tʜɪs ɢɪʀʟ with the abundance of black hair and intense brown eyes, was a great loss to the Sadler's Wells Ballet when she retired in June 1956 to marry an Italian lawyer and live in Rome.

She was born ᴠɪᴏʟᴇᴛᴛᴀ ᴘʀᴏᴋʜᴏʀᴏᴠᴀ in Russia and trained for ballet in the Bolshoi School from the age of eight and a half. Her first leading roles were in Tashkent, where she was evacuated from Moscow, when she was nineteen.

Her English début was at the Royal Opera House, Covent Garden, in 1946, just after she had joined the Sadler's Wells company as a ballerina.

Nathalie
Krassovska

Nathalie Krassovska did fine service for London's Festival Ballet, being with it from the days when it first started as a company proper, and through its early and sometimes difficult seasons.

Particularly, she had been able to step into the Markova roles when Markova was out of action, first through appendicitis and then with a foot injury.

Of her many roles, one of her favourites is *Lac des Cygnes*, which she danced with John Gilpin. That is why I chose this picture.

Nadia
Nerina

IT WAS EASY to see, when I met her, why NADIA NERINA had such a triumph in the name part of *The Firebird*, for there is a flame-like quality about her.

Since she left her home in South Africa to join the Sadler's Wells Ballet School, later to become ballerina with the Company, she has danced leading roles in all the classical ballets. And she has reached a large, popular audience through television.

We took some very gay pictures – because she has gaiety. And then we decided to take this sad one, too.

Belita

Belita, the amazing, posed with the fluid grace so natural to her calling. I loved the rich abundance of her hair which she drew back for this picture.

She is one of those rare creatures who must perfect everything she attempts, though most of us know her as ballerina and ice-skater.

At the age of two she made her first appearance on the stage. She had skated in the Olympics, danced with Dolin, and made a name as a star on ice before she was sixteen.

In Hollywood she became a film actress and as a side-line practised swimming seriously. She became good enough to do a 'short' of underwater swimming and ballet sequences, then to return to London as the star in the Earl's Court Aqua Show.

Since then, she has danced in films, appeared on the stage, on ice, and under water.

Pauline Grant

Gentle and diffident about her work, PAULINE GRANT is among the great ones and never dreams of suggesting it.

She is both inspiring and restful to be with – and to photograph. One cannot classify her – she shines in so many ways. As ballet dancer, choreographer, or director, she is equally absorbed by the job of the moment.

Choreographer for the Glyndebourne Opera Company, she had just returned from a triumph at the Edinburgh Festival when I took this photograph.

She is also choreographer to the Stratford Memorial Theatre, and was responsible for Vera-Ellen's ballet sequences in the film *Let's Be Happy*.

With equal authority she also directs straight plays and ice shows.

Alicia Markova and Anton Dolin

No PARTNERSHIP in modern stage history has brought so much pleasure to ballet-goers as that between ALICIA MARKOVA and ANTON DOLIN.

This picture of them in *Giselle* is my favourite one of them together and one that I think has been admired most. It shows their great artistry and one can sense the perfect partnership that is shown in my portrait.

Anna Roya
and
Myles Marsden

ANNA ROYA AND MYLES MARSDEN photographed in the closing moment of *Giselle* when Albrecht holds the dead Giselle in his arms. This photograph was taken when these two dancers were visiting London during the recent season.

John Gilpin
and
Toni Lander

TONI LANDER AND JOHN GILPIN in one of the *pas de deux* from *Etudes*. This picture was taken during the visit to the studio of Harald Lander, choreographer of *Etudes*, and his wife, together with Anton Dolin, artistic director of London Festival Ballet Annual, and John Gilpin. It is one of a series of photographs of the stars of this amazing ballet taken at the same time.

David Blair

THIS PICTURE of DAVID BLAIR shows his splendid statuesque pose which so much reminded me of the discus thrower. He is the ideal photographic subject and a delight to photograph.

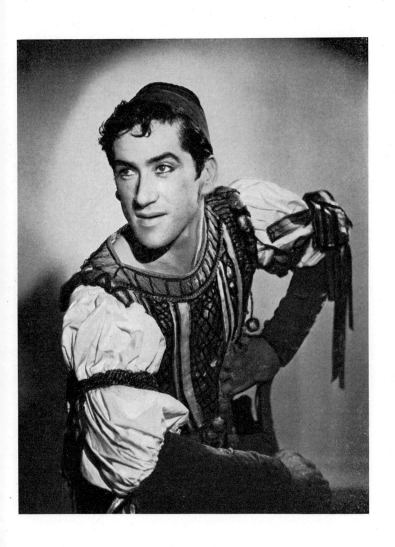

Alexander Grant

HERE IS A YOUNG New Zealander who began dancing when he was nine and won a Royal Academy of Dancing scholarship which entitled him to training in London.

He arrived in England in 1946, joined the Sadler's Wells School and danced for the Sadler's Wells Opera Ballet in the same year.

Now he specializes in character roles and he created the role of Pierre, the French sailor in *Madame Chrysantheme*, and of The Pimp in *The Miraculous Mandarin*.

Bernard Braden

I WAS very conscious of BERNARD BRADEN'S perfect sense of timing when he was sitting for me. And I knew, too, that he was a man of considerable intellect.

Although he is most popularly known as a comedian, I was aware of his potential as a dramatic actor – which he has since shown us that he is – and he said how much he himself enjoys the straight part.

He shares with his wife a liking for tennis and messing about in boats. The latter they do often, from their riverside home at Walton-on-Thames. Bernard Braden and his wife, Barbara Kelly, are one of Canada's great gifts to British radio, for this talented pair had their start on Canada's Pacific coast where they were radio favourites before coming to England.

Robin Day

I HAD ALWAYS felt at home with ROBIN DAY when I watched him on television. His manner was as easy, charming and cosy when I took his photograph.

There was one hitch. He had forgotten his glasses. 'You can't photograph me without them,' he said. 'I'm only known with them on!' So we had to phone his secretary, who would know where to find them. It was while we waited for them to arrive that he explained the vicissitudes of the helpless bachelor lurking behind that happy façade of the confident television announcer!

Radio and Television

Cecil McGivern

Health, as well as mood and other temporary influences, can completely change personality before the camera.

CECIL MCGIVERN had been ill when he first came and he was so highly nervous and tensed up that it was hard to get him to relax. That was during the war, when he was responsible for so many notable programmes from the B.B.C.

He came again (when he had just been made controller of the B.B.C. television programmes in 1950) and he was completely at ease and quite himself – quiet, extremely intelligent and obviously in love with his job.

From Durham, he had been schoolmaster, actor and producer before he joined the B.B.C. In just twenty years he became deputy-director of television.

John Snagge

THE VOICE we have heard describing every Oxford-and-Cambridge boat-race since 1931 arrived to competition from another sound – the engine of a 'doodle bug'.

It cut out and we waited that awful, suspenseful moment till it crashed, uncomfortably near, just over in Green Park.

Then, quite calmly, he sat for this picture.

Apart from the boat-race, of course, John Snagge is head of presentation on the Home Service; has been since 1945.

He has been in broadcasting all his working life, and most of the B.B.C.'s. After he came down from Oxford, he became an assistant station director at twenty, and then moved up as an announcer when the B.B.C. headquarters were still at Savoy Hill.

Lady Kathleen Boyle

Iᴛ ɪsɴ'ᴛ ᴅɪꜰꜰɪᴄᴜʟᴛ to understand why ʟᴀᴅʏ ʙᴏʏʟᴇ is almost universally known as 'Katie'. She encourages an affectionate familiarity.

She is brimful of gaiety, and as at home before the studio camera as she looks on television. I gave her some of my make-up tips, which she said she would use for the benefit of viewers.

There is something Italianate about her, although she is a blue-eyed blonde, and that I have expressed in this picture.

Joan Regan

Sʜᴇ ʜᴀs ʀᴇᴀʟ Irish charm, this young singer, ᴊᴏᴀɴ ʀᴇɢᴀɴ, who rocketed to stardom in 1953 with the TV series 'Quite Contrary'.

The dancing vitality of her movements, the spark of determination in her blue eyes, the way she talked so knowledgeably about her future, left me with little doubt that here is another who came to my studio on the way to greater heights. When she came for this sitting she was currently engaged at the Prince of Wales Theatre, then flying to Germany to entertain the troops before starting pantomime rehearsals for *Jack and the Beanstalk* in Leeds.

I liked the way she made herself cosy in my big armchair – as if she had known it all her life.

Carole Carr

THIS IS CAROLE CARR'S coming-of-age picture. She is as natural and unspoiled as she looks.

Carole came to me first when, at sixteen, she had just become Geraldo's vocalist.

She has the looks – blonde prettiness and such big blue eyes – to become what she was, the Forces sweetheart. What's more, the title is deserving, for she keeps that sweetness which too often becomes brittle in those who find success so young.

Barbara Kelly

HER FRIENDS have told me that they like to see BARBARA KELLY when they are down in the dumps, because she has a sure way of cheering them up.

I saw that brightness in her when she came to the studio, full of life, while she was starring in *The Male Animal*.

As I photographed her, smiling and serious – and highlighted her blonde hair, she talked about husband Bernard Braden and their three children. She believes that family comes first, and consequently she and her husband will never go on long tours together because it means leaving the children.

Richard
Hearne

When he came to me just before a television tour of the United States, I asked him why he covered his handsome face so much with the big glasses and moustache he wears as 'Mr Pastry'. It started thirty years ago and had always been in great demand, he explained.

After the United States trip he was going to Toronto, then down to Melbourne for a show during the Olympic Games, then to make thirty-nine television films which he also scripted.

Brian Reece

I SUPPOSE BRIAN REECE got his first big public as 'P.C. 49' on the radio, but he was, of course, on the stage before the war and, after demobilization, had a good part in Cochran's *Bless the Bride*, which had quite a long run.

Since then he has done a lot of television and stage work, including the Royal Command variety performance in 1955.

But he didn't talk about any of this when he came to the studio. All the time I was photographing him he talked about his children. He was so proud of them, and so completely natural about it,

Edmundo Ros

There is a lilt about EDMUNDO ROS similar to the music he plays. His voice is very deep, his English perfect, and his conversation always animated.

He is very tall, with a great width of shoulder and chest. It was his hands that caught my attention most and I suggested that he took his own, natural position. Then I moved the lights around and took this picture.

Sydney Lipton

Unlike his fellow bandleader, Geraldo, there was nothing apprehensive about SYDNEY LIPTON.

He has considerable ease of manner and movement and a natural conversational flow, which is helpful in catching a fleeting expression.

His is a good face to photograph, firm in contour, with sensitive dark eyes and a mobile mouth. While he was chatting about his pretty wife and daughter Celia – and they were almost the sole subject of his conversation – I got some pictures which pleased us both.

This was his choice – and presumably his wife's and Celia's too!

Geraldo

Mine is an unpredictable profession, because the people who come to the studio make it so. When GERALDO came for his sitting, I was expecting the smooth, blandly smiling bandleader who has so expertly charmed lovers of sweet music with his baton for so long.

One might have thought that I was the dentist, when I asked him to sit down.

'You expect co-operation from your band, don't you?' I inquired – quite gently. He looked rather shaken. Then he gave me a warm smile.

'I expect it, but I don't always get it!' he said.

Then he settled down, and seemed to relax into the mood of the occasion. His pleasant personality came through and we got some very attractive pictures.

Jerry Desmond

THERE WAS a mixture of modesty and confidence about JERRY DESMOND. He was playing with Bob Hope at the time, and I had heard that Bob had called him 'the best straight man in show business'.

While I moved around studying his head – and, oh, that wonderful wavy hair! – he talked about Sid Field, with whom he had linked up in 1942 and worked with on the stage and in films until the great comedian's death.

Since then he has played in films with Arthur Askey and Norman Wisdom – and also in Charlie Chaplin's *King of New York*. Televiewers know him as compère of that quiz, 'The 64,000 Question'.

Jerry is up among the stars, and I think he will stay there. I like a man who can remember his 'epic flops' – the Sid Field films called *London Town* and *Cardboard Cavalier* – as well as his triumphs.

Robert Beatty

ROBERT BEATTY has the rugged charm of the wide open spaces about him – possibly because he comes from Canada.

I realized when we met why this actor has made such a singular success of the 'Man with the Mike' series on B.B.C. television. He is really interested in people, happy to be himself, and there is nothing contrived in his easy manner.

He was very proud of this sweater, which his wife had knitted for him, and I was glad because it suited him so well.

He was most insistent that I should leave all the lines on his forehead.

On TELEVISION I always noticed a natural warmth and friendliness in EUNICE GAYSON – essential attributes for that medium.

She showed the same artless charm when I photographed her. I thought her very pretty indeed – a real brunette with lots of sparkle.

It must be the warm blood in her veins – English, Spanish and Irish-Huguenot – which combined so generously to make her radiant.

At twenty-four, proved in television, films and reviews, she considered herself quite an old trouper, because she began her career on the Scottish music halls ten years before.

'In those days,' she told me, 'I was known as Scotland's Deanna Durbin.'

Eunice
Gayson

Yvonne
Furneaux

Yvonne furneaux is, in my opinion, one of our neglected beauties and I hope that she won't be lost to Hollywood.

She is a true example of brains with beauty, versed in the conversational arts and an interesting, if stern, self-critic of all her work.

Her hair has the lustre of black diamonds and her eyes have the green of jade about them.

I remarked on the richness of her hair. She leaned forward and looked at me with those green eyes.

'But don't you think,' she said seriously, 'that I should have been a redhead?'

Derek Bond

WHEN YOU MEET DEREK BOND you know at once that he is a man's man, with the tweedy companionability of the country pub about him.

As I photographed him I watched his eyes, which are very dark blue. They light up with intense amusement and then are suddenly dark again when his thoughts are serious.

He told me that he started in the theatre learning stage management, and graduated to acting when the producer kindly wrote in two lines for him as a furniture remover.

During the war – he was in the Grenadier Guards, and was awarded the M.C. – he was a prisoner in Germany.

'I swore I'd never go back to Germany in my life,' he said. But his first film was the prisoner-of-war film, *The Captive Heart*, and there he was, back where he had come from.

Dennis Price

FILM STAR DENNIS PRICE came to me during rehearsals with Conchita Montes in the play *To My Love*. He is easy-going, with lots of unassuming charm.

While I was photographing, chatting about the lights in my usual way, I asked him to raise his head.

Rather lazily he did so, remarking: 'Your voice and running commentary are so soothing, they are sending me to sleep. Here am I, due back at rehearsal and I don't want to leave this chair, but just to chat to you!'

The ABOUNDING energy and *bonhomie* in KENNETH HORNE resulted in a photographic session worthy of 'Much Binding in the Marsh'.

'There were a thousand verses written for that catchy little theme song,' he volunteered. 'Written by two very clever chaps, of course.'

'Who were they?' I asked. 'Why Horne and Murdoch,' he grinned.

For all his popular success on radio and television, he doesn't regard himself as a professional. 'Business is my business,' he said. 'The rest is a pleasure and a hobby.'

When I saw him he had become head of the Chad Valley toy company. 'I want kids to have really good toys, and they're going to get them,' said Mr Horne as he smiled good-bye.

Kenneth Horne

Lord
Kemsley

LORD KEMSLEY, proprietor of Kemsley Newspapers, brother of the late Lord Camrose, member of
the illustrious Berry family, was one of the co-operative sitters.

'How quick you are,' he remarked.

'That's because I'm fated to have busy people like you, who never have any time,' I told him.

He laughed and told me that *some* portrait photographers he knew took a couple of hours, which didn't
suit him.

I noted the family likeness in him. He noted his brother's picture on the wall. 'You're going to join him
there,' I told him. And he has.

THE CHAIRMAN of *The Daily Telegraph* is very tall and powerfully built, with a most disarming manner.

He chatted easily about yachting – his great leisure interest – and not at all about newspapers.

I had thought that a Press lord might be reticent and strictly business-like, and told him so.

'Well, I've never been to a photographic studio before,' he told me.

'And quite frankly, I'm rather amused at being photographed by a woman!'

Viscount
Camrose

The Hon.

Michael

Berry

Tʜᴇ ʜᴏɴᴏᴜʀᴀʙʟᴇ ᴍɪᴄʜᴀᴇʟ ʙᴇʀʀʏ, editor-in-chief of *The Daily Telegraph*, walked into the studio as if he were really glad to be there, even though he could only stay for ten minutes.

He was natural and composed – very like his father, the late Lord Camrose.

'But for *The Daily Telegraph*,' I told him, 'I might never have met my husband.' Then I explained that because of an advertisement in *The Daily Telegraph* when I was very young, I went to see the head of an art school where fashion drawing was taught. The head was a Mr Entwistle, who fell in love with me at first sight – and we married two years later.

Michael Berry laughed. 'How very glad I am that my newspaper not only helps people with their careers but also finds them husbands!'

Hᴜɢᴏ ᴡᴏʀᴛʜᴀᴍ has been the diarist, 'Peterborough', of *The Daily Telegraph*, for very many years.

His abrupt way of speaking and his very dry sense of humour have earned him the nickname among some of his friends, they tell me, of 'Old Grumpy'.

He has published many of my pictures in his column and is always frankly delighted when I tell him I have a new one of Sir Winston Churchill.

When I phoned him to say that I had finished a miniature of Sir Winston, he said: 'I am very busy, but I will make a special journey to your studio to see a new picture of that wonderful man.'

He asked, immediately he saw it, for a black-and-white copy, which he published next day.

Hugo Wortham

Eileen Ascroft

Eileen ascroft has appealed to me on many occasions for pictures of beautiful women to illustrate her articles – she is the woman's editor of the *Evening Standard* – and I felt I would like her to sit for me herself.

She was most restful to photograph – a blonde with intensely blue eyes and very expressive hands.

She has a cool and charming manner, and I felt her to be a very practical person, well-endowed for her job of observing the foibles and fashion of the fair sex.

Anne Scott-James

Columnist of the *Sunday Express* Anne scott-james is beautiful and very elegant. Her subject is predominantly fashion, and she is a fine exponent of this sometimes tricky subject.

I found her witty, felt that she had a good mind and that she would not suffer fools gladly, although the soft look about her suggested that she would be kind!

She is a shrewd observer, and she put this talent to great account in her book about the world of glossy magazines, *In the Mink*.

Eve Perrick

COLUMNIST EVE PERRICK has written a lot about me and my photographs. Now the tables are turned.

Unlike her pungent column, she was docile enough when she sat for me, perhaps because she hadn't a pencil in her hand.

I like to show her hands, which are beautiful and integral to her personality. Usually she is cut off at the chin – and a fine, firm chin it is, too – when her picture appears in the *Daily Express*. Here I give you Eve Perrick almost complete.

Ann Temple

I DON'T PRETEND to sense the vocation of all the people who come to the studio. Mood and appearance can be deceptive.

ANN TEMPLE was an exception. It only needed the brief beginnings of conversation to know that her job in life was understanding people.

Her profession is journalism and her 'Human Casebook' column in the *Daily Mail* is famous.

But it is the private and unpublished correspondence that takes most of her time. Thousands of men and women entrust her with their problems and with her alone often lies the great responsibility of guiding them to the right solution.

'I don't really like being photographed, because I think my readers prefer to conjure me up,' she told me. But she sat for this picture and her character is there, in her face.

Malcolm Muggeridge

IN THE FLESH, MALCOLM MUGGERIDGE is much as we know him from television – the assured self-confidence, the preciseness, the incisive voice, the piercing blue eyes. He is a good subject for the photographer.

He saw, in the studio, a picture I had taken of Lord Camrose who, he said, was his last boss (on *The Daily Telegraph*) before he became editor of *Punch*. He told me what a truly great man Lord Camrose was.

Ivor Brown

IVOR BROWN is a very shy man in front of the camera – a quality which, his friends tell me, he shows in other walks of life. He is also probably the most silent sitter I have ever had. His thoughts seemed to be far away. Possibly they were on another book; for, besides being a most distinguished man of the theatre, his literary output – novels, essays, political and philosophical writings – is big and wide-ranging. He did finally venture that he was very busy on another book – about Shakespeare.

Alan Lennox-Boyd

Lɪᴋᴇ ᴍᴀɴʏ ᴘᴏʟɪᴛɪᴄɪᴀɴs, the Colonial Secretary had not a moment to spare – which, I suppose, may be understandable when you think of Cyprus, Aden, and all the other things he had on his plate at the time.

Still, he must find satisfaction in the political life because he got straight into it when he came down from Oxford in the 'twenties, could even be said to have started at Oxford, for he was President of the Union there. And, apart from service with the R.N.V.R. during the war, he has been active in it ever since.

He is very tall and not very easy to photograph but he was pleased with the pictures.

David Marshall

Dᴀᴠɪᴅ ᴍᴀʀsʜᴀʟʟ, lawyer and political leader in Singapore, came to me when he was on a visit to this country to discuss self-government for Singapore.

Reading how Malayanization is driving away so many of his country's top doctors and professors, I have wondered since what he thinks of it now. He is a very forceful character, and, they tell me, a fiery orator, quite something of a stormy petrel. But with me he was quite docile.

I caught him at a moment of uncomplicated concentration, lighting his pipe.

The Late
Kathleen
Ferrier

THE GREAT CONTRALTO came to the studio originally when she was given her first big London engagement – to sing in *The Messiah* at the Albert Hall.

She had, then, a quiet beauty, sweet composure, gentle charm. Love seemed to pour out with her rich speaking voice as it did in her singing. Most of all, she had a radiance about her.

That radiant quality seemed to grow stronger each year. I felt it particularly when I took this picture, just before she died.

The Late
Audrey
Mildmay

I FIRST MET the late AUDREY MILDMAY when she was with the Carl Rosa Opera Company –
and just before she married John Christie.

How superb, I thought, to marry a man who would build an opera house for you, as he did at
Glyndebourne. And how superbly she graced it.

During the war she took her children to Canada and toured there in opera with Sir Thomas
Beecham. It was one of my war jobs to send pictures to her, which she requested by cable.

This portrait shows her as the gracious, charming woman to whom so many owed much. Not
only was she a distinguished singer, but a true patron of the arts.

Jacqueline Delman

IT IS NOT UNIVERSAL – and therefore all the more heart-warming – to find among the successful a continuing appreciation of those who helped them on their way.

JACQUELINE DELMAN, of the beautiful lyric soprano voice, spoke much of her parents.

They were wonderfully understanding, she said, and prepared for her to have many years of training in Italy.

Victoria Sladen

THE APPARENT EASE of fine artistic performance is usually deceptive. It gives one a feeling of encouragement, of humility and, yes, of gratitude to hear in intimate detail the close study and intense effort that goes to produce such delights.

VICTORIA SLADEN, of the blonde hair and the very blue eyes, told me a lot about how hard she worked at her singing. She certainly has a lovely voice.

Adele
Leigh

DESPITE HER HIGH ACHIEVEMENTS in the temperamental world of opera, there are none of the prima donna foibles in ADELE LEIGH.

Her presence is imposing, her personality powerful – I was aware of it the whole time – but it is a friendly aura because of a complete lack of artificiality.

She is a brunette with deep brown eyes, and strong contours. I photographed her almost in profile, a study she particularly likes.

Louis Kentner

Only two days after his arrival in England from Hungary in 1935, Louis Kentner came to my house for a musical evening. He played Beethoven for us and we hoped that he would never stop.

Film director Gabriel Pascal was there – a fellow Hungarian. He has an instinct for great talent. 'Louis has a tremendous future,' he said. How right he was.

When later, I took photographs of him, he was natural and relaxed. Most of all he was happiest at the piano. With his hands on the keyboard – such strong, expressive hands – he was a man absorbed in his art.

Eileen Joyce

When a concert pianist comes to the studio I look instinctively at the hands. One can almost feel the strength of the Eileen Joyce hands even in repose.

She is a very vital person indeed, and gives the impression that she would have made a success in any career she chose. As a sitter she was quiet and pliable.

There is a constant sparkle in her green eyes and something of the schoolgirl in the freckled face framed with red hair.

I have taken many pictures of her for publicity use. I reproduce this private one, taken with her young son.

Albert Ferber

Albert Ferber was a shy guest at our musical parties when he first came here from Switzerland, twenty years ago.

Later, when he came for a sitting, he told me that he was terrified at his small knowledge of English. Then he began to pace up and down the studio, rehearsing the little he knew. He said that he found the atmosphere so warm and reassuring that his fears were quickly vanishing.

He is, of course, a concert pianist of repute, recently playing more often on the continent and in South America. His English, now, is perfect!

Ann Ziegler
and
Webster Booth

The husband/wife singing partnership of anne ziegler and webster booth is evergreen and world famous. In their duets they are the very essence of sweetness and light.

Knowing how critical singers can be – of themselves and of one another – I was most interested to see them in the studio. You can get quite intimate and unexpected glimpses of character when two people are photographed together.

We took a number of pictures – and the songsters were as amenable and charming as they look.

Her highness princess marie louise was eighty-four when she came to my studio. Hers is a regal charm and with it goes that ease of manner which makes meeting her such joy. She was alert and lively, really interested in being photographed. Her hands are so expressive, I let her use them in her own way and just went on taking pictures.

She was interested in my miniatures and later invited me to see her own fabulous collection of the great Victorians.

While she was with me she lighted on the famous Sir Winston portrait and said that she would like to have one.

I shall always remember her driving away in her car, smiling sweetly at the photograph in her hand.

Princess Marie Louise

THE LORD MAYOR OF LONDON, SIR CULLUM WELCH – it was just after his election – was one of my most stimulating visitors.

He sat where he wanted, and looked up with a very bright twinkle in his eye. He seemed completely relaxed, because he was watching with real curiosity what I was about, and there was no self-consciousness in him.

His heavy civic duties apart, he is a very busy practising solicitor in the City, and a company director.

'Hobbies?' he smiled. 'Oh, only my business activities. There's simply no time for any others.'

Sir

Cullum

Welch

SIR JOHN COCKCROFT, director of the Atomic Energy Research Establishment at Harwell, came into my studio like a little boy, with the sweetest smile.

Here was the shy genius, disciple of the great Rutherford, and the man who had been responsible for the first designs of the world's first atom-powered electricity station at Calder Hall – yet he was genuinely surprised when I asked if I might include his picture in my book.

Perhaps such extreme modesty is a natural result of his intimate knowledge of the vast forces in the world around us.

I even had some difficulty in persuading him to raise those intense blue hooded eyes so that I could photograph them.

When he had gone, I wondered whether the happiness in his smile was caused by the thought that on the very next day his great dream would be realized. Because that was the day on which Her Majesty the Queen opened Calder Hall.

Sir

John

Cockcroft

Peter Thorneycroft

About PETER THORNEYCROFT there was none of that exuberant self-confidence that some barristers carry into personal conversation.

For a young man with an important job (President of the Board of Trade since 1951 with Cabinet rank), he had an almost shy quietness.

He is an old Etonian who took up soldiering as a career, then resigned his commission to study law. He became M.P. for Stafford in 1938.

During the war he served with the Royal Artillery and on the Joint Planning Staff. Afterwards he returned to the political front, as Member for Monmouth.

He is another of my pre-election sitters.

It was an honour and a pleasure to have SIR HORACE EVANS, Physician to the Queen, to sit for me.

He is a tall, powerful-looking man, with a very lovely smile. It wasn't a bedside manner smile, but perfectly natural, and I felt how easily he would gain one's absolute confidence.

He sat down wondering whether or not to put on his glasses, which he usually wears.

There was a mock frown, and he said that he did not like being photographed and rarely was.

'In fact, I thoroughly dislike it,' he went on, 'but now that I'm here you'd better do what you can with me.'

Sir Horace Evans

Sir
Cecil
Wakeley

I FELT the professional eminence of SIR CECIL WAKELEY as soon as I met him. It was in his face, his bearing, and in the strong, fine hands.

Among his many appointments, he is chairman of the council of the Imperial Cancer Research Fund, and when he came he was engaged in launching a new appeal.

He is, of course, senior surgeon and director of surgical studies at King's College Hospital, London, and was for five years President of the Royal College of Surgeons.

I noticed that he had a monocle; that one eye didn't take kindly to the lights.

'You've been in the Navy,' I said. I've noticed the overstrained telescope eye on many occasions.

You're quite right,' he answered, and told me that he had been a Surgeon Lieutenant in the First World War and a Surgeon Rear-Admiral in the Second! He is still surgeon-consultant to the Royal Navy.

Christina Foyle

I LOOKED FORWARD to meeting CHRISTINA FOYLE — someone whose mind, I felt, must be a great library of knowledge!

We talked about books, of course, and about the changing tastes of library subscribers. While I busied myself with my lights she told me something of the authors whose reputations she has helped to launch through her famous literary lunches.

Hers is a strong, intelligent face with clear, direct eyes and a quick responsive smile. The look of a woman who knows what she is about, and who does it well.

IT WAS AS President of the Incorporated Society of Fashion Designers that LADY PAMELA BERRY came to my studio. While I have little time to attend the shows, I have a professional interest in clothes and so was curious to meet her.

She was so unobtrusively well-dressed for her sitting that I quite forgot what she did wear!

What I felt at once, and remember, was her vitality, her enormous vitality. Her brown eyes are deep and dynamic, and her skin has an olive glow.

She told me that fashion had always been one of her loves, and so she accepted the honour of the Presidency. I could well imagine her competence and flare in organizing the London shows,

Lady
Pamela
Berry

The Hon.
Iris Peake

LADY-IN-WAITING to Her Royal Highness Princess Margaret, the HON. IRIS PEAKE seemed to have just those qualities of character which one imagines such an appointment demands.

She was a very easy and charming sitter – conveying the impression that all this was rather pleasant.

Hers is a quiet personality, but with it goes an abundant sense of humour, which one glimpses quickly in her grey eyes.

Her movement is graceful – she is tall and slender – and a turn of the head, a gesture of the hand, is pleasing to watch.

Diana
Barnato Walker

DIANA BARNATO WALKER is a very accomplished sportswoman who remains essentially feminine. Like her well-known father, Squadron-Leader Woolfe Barnato, who was an air ace of the First World War, she is a keen pilot. She is also a horsewoman, skilled in yachting and a brilliant hostess.

Add to that her very vivid personality – she is so alive and warm – her exquisite dress sense, and you will know what I have tried to capture in this photograph.

Ellen Anderson

ELLEN ANDERSON, a petite brunette, with a direct and friendly personality, is editor of *Books of the Month*.

Book publishing is her great interest, and she spends most of her spare time reading manuscripts for publishing houses.

'That's been my business most of my life and I think I know what makes a good book,' she told me.

Hers is a transatlantic experience. A Canadian, she was editor of the book publishers, McClelland & Stewart, in Toronto. Later she spent some time in New York, free-lancing among the publishing houses, before coming here to widen her already considerable horizon.

Lady Portman

THERE HAVE BEEN many requests for copies of my photographs for social and publicity reasons, but only once to aid the police.

LADY PORTMAN, distinguished wife of Viscount Portman of Chalfont St Giles, came for her sitting wearing the magnificent jewels which are shown in her picture.

A few days later her home was burgled and these exquisite jewels were among the stolen valuables. Lady Portman's insurance company rang me to ask for copies to circulate for identification purposes.

I learned, during our sitting, that Lady Portman is a great dog lover, and a most knowledgeable one, with a special penchant for dachshunds and bloodhounds.

Michael Charnley

THIS BRILLIANT YOUNG MAN, MICHAEL CHARNLEY, is not only distinguished as a choreographer for ballet, but as the director of two of the most successful modern reviews of the West End stage, *Intimacy at 8.30* and *For Amusement Only*.

He came to me soon after his most controversial work, *Homage to a Princess* which he created for the wedding of Prince Rainier and Grace Kelly to music specially written by the American jazz composer, Stan Kenton.

His first choreography for a major ballet company, *Symphony for Fun*, was for the Festival Ballet. It showed a gay and vital sense of colour and a fine dance invention knit splendidly with the music.

Then for the Coronation season he did *Alice in Wonderland*, a ballet which has been performed in many parts of the world to the delight of thousands who find new joy and life given to Lewis Carroll's immortal story.

I always admire a man who gains his success by coming up the hard way – which Michael Charnley most certainly did.

Aₗₜₕₒᵤ𝒈ₕ ʜᴇ ɪꜱ a pianist and composer by profession, ᴍᴀʀᴄ ᴀɴᴛʜᴏɴʏ is, above all, a devotee of the art of conversation.

'It's an almost dying art and in my small way I want to revive it,' he told me. And so it is that any week-end one finds his London flat full of people talking, with only the clink of tea and coffee cups – no alcohol – as background music.

In the 1930s Marc Anthony composed light music for Charlot and Cochran. The music for the Markova-Dolin ballet, *Ballerina in the Moonlight* was his. Few men possess his elfin charm, his sparkling wit, his skill at picturing in words some almost-forgotten moment cherished by many stage folk; few have his complete sincerity. He has one of the widest circles of friends of any man I know.

When he came to my studio his talk ranged through ballet, books, theatre, while I photographed him and I caught him at a characteristically intense moment.

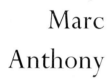

Marc
Anthony

Tilly Losch

THE EXOTIC, ENCHANTING TILLY LOSCH.
Max Reinhardt found her in Vienna and took
her to Berlin to dance in his productions there.
C. B. Cochran brought her to London and
America to star in his revues. And we remember
her dancing with Dolin at Covent Garden in
Die Fledermaus in the 1930s.

Although she is now living in the United States,
and has been for some time, I can always recall
her as she was on the day that I took this
photograph.

There is an elusive, timeless grace and glamour
about her; she is somehow the spirit of the dance.

Mrs Gerald Legge

I WAS QUITE curious to meet the young and
energetic MRS GERALD LEGGE, whose looks and
activities and undoubted intelligence make her
one of the most publicized members of Society.
Frankly, I wondered in my maturity how this
recently-appointed Westminster City Councillor
and I would get along.
She came in so prettily, with her councillor's
robes on one arm and a beautiful pink crinoline
frock on the other.
She was smiling and bright-eyed and happy and
talked to me about her mother (novelist
Barbara Cartland) as she donned her robes.
I sat her in an armchair in which she at once
relaxed and her blue eyes danced towards the
camera. Despite the robes, she was a picture of
soft femininity, and her hat was almost pert.
I photographed her, too, in her gorgeous
crinoline; and I have taken her portrait several
times since.
But I reproduce the young City Councillor
because she was my most pleasant surprise.

Maharanee of Jaipur

PEOPLE HAVE sometimes asked me if I ever grow tired of beautiful faces. I think they confuse beauty with what I call doll-like prettiness, in which case my answer would be yes.

But beauty – well, here is beauty in the MAHARANEE, and one could never grow tired of that.

Hers takes one's breath away. And, of course, it is world famous. She brought a hush and a glow into my studio, and bliss to my artist's eye.

Her features are perfect – there is no more to say about that. Her skin is palest olive and her gleam of black hair enhances it. Add to that the Eastern serenity, that mysterious inner something which is, I suppose, the true secret of beauty, and you have what I saw that day in my studio – this picture.

Her Highness
The Princess Bera

PRINCESS BERA has the colouring for a Leonardo to paint. Hair of true copper colour, deepest sapphire blue eyes, complexion of palest olive. The perfect balance of this exquisite colouring actually reproduces in black and white. She has lustre in her voice, a delicious sense of humour, a natural grace.

Beyond her beauty and her intellect, she is memorable to me because I have never before seen anyone dressed in pure gold. Her fabulous Benares sari, I thought, must be of the rarest silk. 'Oh, no,' she smiled, 'it is of pure gold, hammered and hammered until it is so . . .'

Princess Bera is the daughter-in-law of the Nizam of Hyderabad.

She is also straight from Arabian Nights.

Helen, Duchess of Northumberland

Helen, DUCHESS OF NORTHUMBERLAND, was Mistress of the Robes to the Queen Mother during her reign as Queen. Daughter of the Duke of Richmond and Gordon, she married Earl Percy, afterwards Duke of Northumberland. I found her so gracious, with the charming dignity of the truly well-bred woman. Physically, apart from the delicate features and effortless, regal movement, I remember her hair, red-gold hair, now turning to silver.

The Duchess of Argyll

It WAS IN the nineteen-thirties that I first saw the DUCHESS OF ARGYLL. She was then Margaret Whigham, débutante, and generally thought to be the most lovely of them all. As Mrs Charles Sweeney she was a famous society hostess. She was almost never written about without the prefix 'beautiful'.

The Duchess retains her beauty. If anything, it is enhanced. She is always elegant and perfectly poised. The hat she wears for this picture – a tricorn which fashion can never date – is characteristic of her taste.

Olive,
Lady Baden Powell

WOMEN WITH THE true quality of leadership are comparatively few. LADY BADEN POWELL is undisputedly one of them.

She has an air of distinction and quiet authority; she gives to her uniform a womanly softness.

As World Chief Guide in the vast association of scouts and guides to which her husband, the late Lord Baden Powell had devoted all his energy and resource, she is a woman who does not know the meaning of spare time.

She is a perpetual traveller, fostering the cause she loves in many lands.

It is her great joy that the movement is ever on the increase. She told me that there were half a million members in this country, and about three and a half million throughout the world.

Mary,
Countess Howe

I WAS MUCH amused when the COUNTESS asked me to take 'some really glamorous' pictures of her. She is so wonderful anyway. 'I will do my best,' I told her.

Then I draped her in my own black velvet to give the right contrast to her perfect, glowing alabaster skin.

There is a particular and professional interest for me in photographing, in her maturity, a woman who has always been known as a famous beauty.

The Countess's fair hair is greying now, but it retains the sheen it always had. The exquisite modelling of her face and the perfect poise of her head can never change.

That is, perhaps, the finesse of beauty.

Signor Pietro Annigoni

Aɴɴɪɢoɴɪ arrived with his favourite model, Juanita Forbes, and dominated me and the studio – at first. He is almost larger than life in physical and mental stature.

'Go away while I photograph Juanita,' I said.

'No,' he told me, 'I'm admiring your work and not saying a word.'

When I photographed him he was quiet for a while, then could not resist asking me to move my lights as he wished, which I did. When he saw the pictures, he told me that he preferred those which I took my way.

'I don't know anything about photography,' he admitted. But we agreed that as a painter uses brush and colour, so I, as a photographer, use my lights.

W<small>E WERE TRYING</small> to decide where this portrait of the late A<small>NNE</small> C<small>RAWFORD</small> should appear, when news was received of her passing.

With her death, stage, radio, film and television have all lost a brilliant and charming actress. She was voted last year the leading T V actress in the land and had built up a very large audience in that medium. Her West End appearances and those on films revealed a depth of artistry that set her apart.

This simple portrait is now included here, for Miss Crawford was indeed distinguished in the life of the nation by her many other associations apart from the entertainment world.

The Late
Anne
Crawford

Gladys
Young

As to millions of radio listeners, GLADYS YOUNG has for years been a Voice to me – an unforgettable one.

Had I not known that it was she who walked into the studio, I would have recognized her the moment she spoke.

She has the clear, pure diction that tells of long training in voice production, and a modulation quite distinctive to herself.

I felt that the voice portrayed the woman. She has mature good looks, greyish hair that becomes her, a slight figure and an attractive trimness.

Her sincerity is unmistakable and her love of the Spoken Word, as the B.B.C. calls it, quite intense. That, I expect, is why for so long she has devoted her considerable acting talents exclusively to sound radio, for which I, among her many listeners, am grateful.

Esmond Knight and Nora Swinburne

The marriage partnership of ESMOND KNIGHT and NORA SWINBURNE belongs to their private life rather than to the stage, although they are both artists of the theatre.

I am among the many who admire the nobility of Esmond Knight in tackling the tragedy of his last-war blindness. After meeting him, I felt that his complete lack of bitterness may have contributed to the partial regaining of his sight. His wife, Nora Swinburne, is a true English beauty, and so intensely feminine. While I photographed her I was absorbed not only by the perfection of her features, but by the real music in her soft voice.

Madame Haggloff

Madame HAGGLOFF, wife of the Swedish Ambassador in London, told me that she was a pure Roman. She certainly has the classic Roman nose.

I am fascinated by her hair which she alters so cleverly to suit her mood. She has perfect dress sense. Her clothes are never more important than she is. One feels she has that fashion instinct which too many women lack – of being able to look into the mirror to see if some accessory might be taken off, rather than to add an extra.

Here you see her with her son, Axel – who is also beautiful.

Sir Laurence and Lady Olivier

Tʜɪꜱ ᴄʜᴀʀᴍɪɴɢ ᴘʜᴏᴛᴏɢʀᴀᴘʜ of ꜱɪʀ ʟᴀᴜʀᴇɴᴄᴇ ᴏʟɪᴠɪᴇʀ and ᴠɪᴠɪᴇɴ ʟᴇɪɢʜ is my
favourite of them together.

The sultan of muscat and oman, His Highness Said bin Taimur, is the thirteenth of his dynasty in the Sultanate. The dynasty, to which the Sultan of Zanzibar also belongs, goes back more than two hundred years.

With his warm personality and his red turban, he seemed to have stepped straight out of *The Arabian Nights*. He said he wanted a picture from the photographer who had taken Sir Winston Churchill and Sir Anthony Eden.

A photographer's work finds its way to all sorts of places. It is a particular pleasure to me to think of mine reposing in the Sultan's palace away down there in the eastern corner of Arabia.

The

Sultan

of

Muscat

and

Oman

One hundred and sixty-nine

Ernest George Entwistle

I FIRST MET ERNEST when he had a school of fashion drawing and I went along as a pupil. We were married in 1913.

It was under his tuition in drawing and colour values that I developed as a painter of miniatures and later he was to train both our sons in art.

After closing down his school in the First World War, when he served in the Royal Flying Corps, he built it up again, and then in 1942 we started the photographic studio, with Ernest looking after the business side.

So through all these years we have worked side by side and Ernest is almost as well known to my sitters as I am.

Clive Entwistle

MY STUDIO and the flat above it were once old stable buildings. My architect son, CLIVE ENTWISTLE, remodelled the whole place for me. As an architect he has worked with the great Frenchman Le Corbussier, and he has translated some of his works.

He is also an engineer, and was research assistant to Sir Frank Whittle during the development of the first jet-prop engine.

Now he has added industrial design and manufacturing to his professional achievements. I am happy to say that he is thinking of the housewife and concentrating on domestic equipment which will make her life more easy and efficient!

Florence Entwistle

This is a self-portrait of Florence Entwistle, better known to her host of sitters as VIVIENNE.

The photographs in this book offer their own tribute to a fine artist. – *The Editor*.

Antony Beauchamp

I DON'T MIND being asked that invidious question: 'Who is your worst sitter?' I can answer in honesty: 'My son.'

Because he himself is a famous photographer – he changed his name when we became 'rivals' – he knows all the secrets of camera technique. I feel him watching me, anticipating my lighting tricks, being inwardly critical – or perhaps amused!

He is, in fact, a photogenic subject. I took my favourite picture of him when he returned lean and sun-bronzed from four war years in the Far East where he was with Mountbatten and with Wingate's Chindits as Crown photographer.

Being my son – and perhaps because he is now a film producer – he did not agree with my choice, so we show this picture instead.

The Late

Baron

Dᴜʀɪɴɢ ᴛʜᴇ ʟᴏɴɢ ʏᴇᴀʀs that I knew sᴛɪʀʟɪɴɢ ʙᴀʀᴏɴ ɴᴀʜᴜᴍ, I never at any time heard him express an envy of another photographer.

Towards the end of the Second World War, Baron and I were neighbours, and he came to our home often. We teased each other a lot about our clientele, but always in the friendliest way. He was an artist whose warm smile and gentleness will always be missed. I am proud that I photographed Baron before his death and that I can give him a place of honour in my book. It is fitting that he should be the last in this book composed of the portraits of the many famous people I have photographed.